I *CAN* FINISH COLLEGE

I CAN FINISH COLLEGE

The Overcome *Any* Obstacle and Get Your Degree Guide

MARCIA Y. CANTARELLA, PHD
FOREWORD BY JOHN ROSE

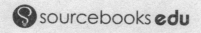

Sourcebooks and the colophon are registered trademarks of Sourcebooks, Inc.

Published by Sourcebooks EDU, an imprint of Sourcebooks, Inc.
P.O. Box 4410, Naperville, Illinois 60567-4410
(630) 961-3900
Fax: (630) 961-2168
www.sourcebooks.com

Originally published in January 2011 by lulu.com.

Library of Congress Cataloging-in-Publication Data

Cantarella, Marcia Y.
  I can finish college : the overcome any obstacle and get your degree guide / Marcia Y. Cantarella ; foreword by John Rose.
    p. cm.
  Includes bibliographical references and index.
  (trade paper : alk. paper) 1. First-generation college students—United States. 2. People with social disabilities—Education (Higher)—United States. 3. Educational attainment—United States. 4. Study skills—United States—Handbooks, manuals, etc. 5. College student orientation—United States—Handbooks, manuals, etc. 6. Degrees, Academic—United States—Handbooks, manuals, etc. I. Title.
  LC4069.6.C36 2012
  378.1'982–dc23
                                    2012020533

Printed and bound in Canada.
WC 10 9 8 7 6 5 4 3 2 1

To Francesco and our children and their children and all children

The one who asks questions doesn't lose his way.

—Akan Proverb

Because we don't always want to be stupid, uninformed, or belittled, we don't like to ask questions. For some reason, we think that we are supposed to know everything. When we don't, we don't let anyone know. Questions are not a sign of ignorance. They are an indication that you are broadening your scope, sharpening your skills, improving your capabilities. Inquiries indicate humility, the willingness to serve, share, and support. Questions keep you on track, define and broaden your boundaries, and remove limitations. Questions put you in touch and keep you in touch. Questions create and build resources, both natural and human, which can be very useful when there is no one around to answer your question. Your ego, the nasty little voice that is overconcerned with what other people think, will tell you not to ask questions. Tell ego to shut up, and then ask what you need to know. Who? What? Where? When? How? Why?

—Ayanla Vanzant
Acts of Faith: Daily Meditations for People of Color

CONTENTS

FOREWORD

Every year many thousands of students and their parents struggle with the question of whether they have good-quality information to make informed decisions about college, academic, or career interests. The odyssey begins with finding the "right" college and asking questions such as "What do I really need to know?" and "Can I get as good an education at a public school as at an elite private university?" Once students are in college, their questions continue to multiply about finances, courses, courseloads, specialized programs, internships, cocurricular and extracurricular activities, and how to build a portfolio or skills and experiences that distinguish them from other applicants for graduate or professional school or for that first job after college.

To answer these questions, parents and students wade through countless reference and resource materials, look at the annual reviews by *U.S. News and World Report* and *Princeton Review*, talk to admissions officers, advisors, and counselors, and share information and impressions with classmates and their parents. Ultimately they make an "informed" decision. But for too many there remains the nagging question, "Did I know what I really needed to know?"

This question need no longer plague students or parents, because Marcia Y. Cantarella has distilled all the "inside" knowledge and perspective from her years of experience as a college administrator and dean into a book that answers not only all the common questions, but also the questions that most students do not even think about until too late in the process.

Dr. Cantarella has served at Ivy League, private, and public institutions and has a depth of knowledge about college admissions practices, policies, and protocols that is truly exceptional. She has served on many admissions and pipeline-program committees. I have personally benefited from her keen insights into the distinguishing characteristics driving student motivation and guiding administrator decision making.

Her appreciation of the academic rigors of various disciplines and her unerringly accurate evaluation of student talent and motivation have allowed her to pair students with opportunities for academic programs, scholarships, and fellowships that have been consistently good fits. She is, therefore, an invaluable resource for those who want a perspective on the mounds of publicly available data and analysis. If you want to hear from an insider who is vested in student success, who tells you what you need to know to make intelligent decisions without fear of omitting important information, then you need to read—and use—Dr. Cantarella's book, *I Can Finish College*.

—John Rose
Dean for Diversity and Compliance
Hunter College of The City University of New York

ACKNOWLEDGMENTS

This book is the product of many hands. I refer not just to the team that has helped me, in the past few months, bring it to a published reality, but also to the family that inspired me and the colleagues who empowered me—and finally to the students who shared their lives with me.

I was born to a family of educators and leaders, including my paternal grandparents, Whitney Young Sr. and Laura Ray Young, who ran the Lincoln Institute in Kentucky, so that young Black men and women could find a path to success through education. My late father, Whitney Young Jr., opened doors to educational opportunity for all poor and disenfranchised peoples. My aunts Arnita Boswell and Dr. Laura Young Love were pioneering professors at the Universities of Chicago and Louisville, respectively, and my mother was on the faculty at Spelman College.

My colleagues at New York University, Princeton, Metropolitan College of New York, and Hunter College have given me the opportunity to serve, to lead, and to learn from extraordinary students who have survived college and who thrive today. Their stories inform much of this book. Special thanks to Deans William Long at NYU, Nancy Malkiel at Princeton, and John Rose at Hunter College.

Then there are the students who have sat before me over the twenty years that I have had the honor to serve them. They have come with aspirations, frustrations, disasters, and joys. We have strategized together to achieve goals or solve problems. We have celebrated wins large and small, from grades achieved to fellowships won, and now often marriages and children. Students are the real reason for this book, and I am so grateful that so many have allowed me to use their stories and their wisdom in it.

The fact that so many had similar situations challenging them across a wide array of schools told me that a vast number of students everywhere shared their concerns. As a consultant to colleges and programs now, I again come across the same scenarios, played out across many campuses, validating what I first heard in my offices: students telling me what they did not know and needed to know.

Finally, there is the team that has made *I* Can *Finish College* a reality. Cheryll Y. Greene, the editor, has understood the intention of the book from the start and worked to maintain the tone and bring clarity to every line. Leah Lococo, the designer, has been professional, caring, and insightful about the feel of the book and its appeal to a diverse audience. I am also grateful to Jerilyn Famighetti, the copy editor, and Nila Gilkin, the indexer, for their significant contributions. Morolake Thompson, who came to me as a student intern from the Futures and Options program, has been a gift. She represents the students for whom this book is intended. She has been invaluable in creating the website, much of the marketing strategy, and lots of lists. I wish her all the very best as she goes off to Hamilton College.

My friends have been my cheerleaders, and my kids—now adults—have suffered having their stories told to student audiences for years and now put in print. None of this would have been possible without the faith that my late husband, Francesco Cantarella—himself the child of college professors Helene and Michele Cantarella and a former trustee of the City University system—placed in me every day of our twenty-eight years together. Thank you all.

INTRODUCTION:
WHY DO YOU NEED THIS BOOK?

You have worked hard preparing to go to college. You know that you need a degree to succeed and to achieve your goals, and perhaps in order to contribute to your family and community. You want to see yourself in one of those pictures of happy graduates celebrating a hard-won achievement. And you don't want to get derailed along the way—you want to *finish* college. This book is meant to help you get there. You will also learn, I hope, that the smartest, most mature individuals are the ones who ask questions and use every tool available in order to move ahead.

After nearly twenty years in higher education, teaching and otherwise engaging with college students in many capacities, I have learned that despite our efforts at orientation via websites or first-year workshops or handbooks, students still don't know all they need to know about how these institutions work and how to navigate them. Most often, what may seem like something that's just inside information you don't need turns out to be exactly what's needed when a student is in crisis. That's when we find ourselves saying, "But didn't you know…?" And they didn't. You can probably sympathize: You're so relieved to be in college that the flurry of advice in the first crazy days, weeks, and months has swept over your head. Moreover, many matters haven't been presented with you in mind.

Most schools offer first-year orientations and informational websites, but they may assume that you're coming to college with more awareness than you actually have about the inside workings of higher education institutions. You may be the first in your family to attend college, so you aren't familiar with the kinds of school traditions and stories that circulate within college-trained families—and even students from those families may not have all the information they need. You may not know which questions to ask. You may feel embarrassed about asking them, because you assume you're the only one without the information. Or you think consulting the catalog or school website in a cursory way or asking a senior student will suffice. You may be a returning student who has been away from school for some time. You may even mistakenly think you already know how to handle whatever comes up.

This book is meant to answer the questions you don't even know you have, regardless of what year you're in or where you come from. It can be read cover to cover, but you may find it more useful if you read it on an as-needed basis. Look at the chapters that address the issues you're facing right now, or use the contents page or index to find specific information as you need it. This book will *not* take the place of your specific school's catalog, website, or advisors, but may assure that you use these aids most wisely and effectively. Every school is unique, and each has its own variations in rules, but there are commonalities that cut across almost all of them, and these are the issues we will address here.

What kinds of situations am I talking about? Let's take email, for example. It is likely that your school will give you a college email address, but you may want to continue using your hotstuff@myself.com personal address. So you don't open or pay attention to campus emails. That is a mistake! Find out why as you read this book. Also find out the answers to questions such as

- Can grades be appealed?
- Do you have to major in bio to go to medical school?
- Can you march at graduation if you're missing a credit (or two)?
- Can you make friends with your professors?

- Should you join clubs or just focus on your studies?
- Is it good or bad news if the dean's office calls?
- How do you relate to your parents or other family members when you're in college?
- Can you work twenty hours a week and still get good grades?

This is just a small sample of the questions you might not yet know you have. You and your family have invested so much in getting you to college; don't let the little things—or the big ones—trip you up along the way. As you use this book to help you navigate the college pathways, you will find "Cautionary Tales" throughout, which are based on true stories of pitfalls students have faced (names changed, in most cases, to protect the innocent). These stories illustrate the lessons you will find in each chapter. Similarly, stories throughout show students who successfully faced challenges that could have been barriers to graduating. Use these stories as tools to help make your journey clearer and smoother as you progress toward completing your college degree.

Experts have recognized that students who succeed in college have what is known as emotional intelligence, sometimes called EQ. This means that they

- Are resilient
- Know how to face obstacles
- Manage time
- Take advantage of resources
- Build networks
- Become self-aware
- Become self-confident
- Learn from every experience (good or bad)
- Focus on personal aspirations
- Take responsibility for themselves

These qualities are not limited to the rich or privileged—often students who come from difficult backgrounds, marked by struggle, possess these qualities in abundance. The tools they use to survive in life can be the factors that lead to success in college. Interestingly, these are the same qualities that employers seek. The information, advice, and strategies for success in this book are based on what I have learned from directing programs and initiatives that have helped students develop just these skills and characteristics, and more important, on what I have learned from students themselves.

I have also learned, through the years, that almost half of the students who get into college do not graduate. You want to be among the winners, and you can be! You can succeed and finish college if you learn how these institutions work and how they can work for you. This book is meant to help you do just that. The goal is your graduation.

�=➤

Let *I* Can *Finish College* be your guide to overcoming any obstacle and getting your degree. It is organized to take you through the central questions, experiences, processes, and relationships that you'll encounter in the years leading up to—and even a bit beyond—graduation.

Chapter 1, "Why College?" helps you focus on the importance of knowing what your goals are and on claiming them as your own. Going to college right after high school may not be right for everyone. Some young persons need to take time away from school; others need a purely vocational focus; some are only doing what they've been told they should do. But if you know you have the capacity to do the work and your goals will require an undergraduate degree, or higher, then college is the next right step. (If you're starting the process without a high school diploma, you'll find information about earning your GED.) This chapter helps you clarify your thoughts and plans, and it suggests types of schools to match your goals, aptitudes, style, and resources. Then, with greater confidence, you can delve into the many books and websites designed to help you choose specific schools and navigate the application process. And if you're not a U.S. citizen, look for the information and advice here about your options.

"Financing Your Education," chapter 2, suggests financial considerations in planning for college, points you toward the essential steps in the federal loan process, and suggests additional sources for funds. A sample budget helps you plan.

Chapter 3, "Get Going: The Processes," introduces you to the registrar's and bursar's offices. You'll find out what you need to know about simplifying the processes of choosing your required and elective classes and staying on track to graduate. You'll also learn about the role of the advising offices and how the faculty fits in.

How to select your courses, your major, and your electives are topics explored in chapter 4, "Which Courses?" You'll find essential answers to key questions: What are core curricula, and why do schools use them? Why are there required courses? What do placement tests tell the college and you? What are the differences among course levels such as 100 or 300? How many courses can or should you take? How do you know if a course is a "good" or a "gut" (undemanding) course? Are easy classes better than hard classes? How do you survive hard classes that you can't escape? What is the impact of transferring from one school to another?

Chapter 5, "The Professors," tells you what the faculty really does, whether your professors should be your friends, how they can be helpful, and how you can approach them. The chapter addresses other crucial issues: What if you have a disagreement with a professor—where do you go then? Can you disagree about a grade? What is "academic integrity," and why is it such a big deal? How do you get a letter of recommendation from a professor? How do you get a faculty mentor, and what does that mean? What if you are sexually harassed by a professor (or administrator or graduate student)?

Chapter 6 looks at "Your People." Who are they? Life during college is full of relationships—roommates, girl- or boyfriends, friends, fraternity or sorority members, club members, employers, families close and far, and, of course, faculty and administrators. How do these people become your support team, instead of adversaries or obstacles? What is the appropriate role for these people who make demands on you during college? What if you are an older student—are these relationships any different?

Chapter 7, "Transitions," takes you through each year, from freshman to senior, showing you how to deal with the expectations and changes that come up, leading up to graduation. Find out the pitfalls and opportunities in each of these years; the best time to take advantage of opportunities such as internships, fellowships, or study abroad; and when and how it is best to transfer to another school if you want to do that.

It seems like there is never enough time. "Time Management and Study Skills," chapter 8, provides you with advice on how to balance the demands of coursework, a job, a relationship, leadership roles, and playtime—and still have a 3.9 GPA without a 140 IQ. There are plenty of students who have achieved this, and through the stories in this book they will speak to you directly about what they do to succeed—their tips are some of the best around.

Chapter 9, "When It Feels Like a Crisis," zeroes in on those moments of panic when you feel you can't cope (you can't get your paper done in time, you've missed several classes in a row, your roommate is drunk most of the time, your family is crumbling). You need to know what the counseling center does. What are your privacy rights? What can you expect or ask for from the deans, advisors, resident and peer advisors, chaplains, health center, and faculty?

Is college the dress rehearsal for the rest of your life? Chapter 10, "Preparing for Life after College," considers this question and helps you think ahead. Once you leave the relatively safe space of college, where mistakes may have less severe consequences, how will you handle yourself? How do you prepare for an independent life? This chapter suggests how you can build toward a career while you're in school and how you should think about the world of work or graduate school and prepare for it in practical terms.

You've made it through! Chapter 11, "Graduation!" tells you how to make the most of this, the wonderful event that celebrates your achievement, for yourself and your loved ones.

It's important to hold on to your college network. In chapter 12, "Being an Alumnus," find out the way to do this through your college's alumni association. Should you be involved? The association asks you for money, but what's in it for you? As an alumnus, can you still use college resources? Can older alumni support you in your goals? How do you stay connected with your classmates, and what's the advantage in doing that? Is the association a way to connect with current and future students like you?

The saying goes, Knowledge is power, but when you enter college, it feels as though both those attributes are in the hands of everyone but you. Wherever you are in your educational journey through college, you can find helpful and necessary information here. This book is meant to shift some of that knowledge and power back to you, so you can find your way through the processes and procedures of finishing college and getting your degree— and find your way to the persons who can help. The knowledge and power belong to you.

Chapter 1
WHY COLLEGE?

This chapter is meant to help you confirm that you're making, or have made, the right decisions about college. These years can be a time of transition between adolescence and adulthood, especially if you're between the ages of seventeen and twenty-one. College at age seventeen, in a traditional setting, is not right for everyone. Given the costs of higher education, it is important to think through the options that may be available, to ensure that you get your money's worth out of the experience. If you are not yet in college and you are trying to decide whether higher education is right for you or which school might be, or you're thinking about a transfer, then read this chapter. If you're feeling that you're in the right place, then you may want to move to another part of the book.

A Story: Kimberly

Kimberly is a beautiful, poised young woman who was a model in high school and then began a retail business that did very well. She kept pushing college to the background until she found herself in her early twenties without a degree and uncertain that she wanted to continue running her small store. Modeling had lost its luster as well, and she found that her other options were closed off without a college degree. While Kim had done well enough to sustain herself, her mother was a single parent and couldn't help with money for college. So Kim chose to apply to a public college, which was affordable.

Her first year was a struggle, as she was not sure what she wanted to study, and she felt older than the other students. Sociology caught her attention, however, and she also began to get involved in student government. Soon her skills and poise as a speaker, derived from her time outside the college setting, brought her to the attention of some of the college deans and even the president. She was offered the chance to speak to alumni, to participate in events, and to take special internships. Her networks grew, and so did her opportunities.

Kim is now a fashion executive, using what she learned both before and during her college years. Her job is the direct result of networks and opportunities provided by her college experience. Taking time to pursue a passion before college did not derail Kim's dreams, but college enhanced them and her range of options.

WHY COLLEGE?

First, you should understand that college training has a much greater significance today than it did earlier. More than a century ago, work most often involved physical labor. As the twentieth century progressed, however, more and more work became administrative or managerial, though physical skills were still in demand. Following World War II and in the 1950s in particular, as a bigger share of the population had access to free public high schools, workers developed skills more exclusively suited for office work. At present we are clearly in a service- and knowledge-based economy, where the skills developed through a college education are the ones driving both economic and personal growth.

But is now the right time for you to attend, and what schools might best suit your circumstances? Getting through college successfully may actually depend on your being at the right school in the first place. The College Board, the preeminent organization connecting students to colleges, lists nearly four thousand accredited colleges and universities. The options are nearly limitless. You should choose based on who you are and what is right for you (not on what your parents did or didn't do, or what your friends are doing).

ASSESS YOUR NEEDS

Check the descriptions below and match them to your situation to find the strategy best suited to helping you find the most appropriate type of college for you. For some of you, more than one scenario might be appropriate.

Info: Choosing a College

There are many books and resources to help you choose a school. A couple of the best are the College Board site (**http://www .collegeboard.com**) and **http://www.Petersons.com**, which will have information on particular schools of interest to you, as well as Boyer and Boyer's *Smart Parent's Guide to Colleges: The 10 Most Important Factors for Parents and Students When Choosing a College,* or *Choosing a College* by Thomas Sowell.

Loves Learning

When you were in high school you loved learning and being part of a community where others did too. That is the first clue that you are college material. You may not have admitted your love to others for fear of being considered geeky, but if in your soul you reveled in the ideas exchanged in your classes, then college could feel as if you're in a big candy store. You will be among many others who feel the way you do, and you'll have access to faculty who can feed your desire to learn and engage in new ideas. Being smart is cool in college.

If this is you, you have the most options available to you. One of the best is the traditional liberal arts college, which varies greatly in size. There are small stand-alone colleges, such as Haverford in Pennsylvania, Carleton in Minnesota, or Agnes Scott or Spelman in Georgia, are other options. Colleges of this type grant bachelor's degrees (Bachelor of Arts or Bachelor of Science, abbreviated to BA or BS). There are small ones that are part of huge university complexes, such as Harvard College, the College of Arts and Sciences at New York University, or Pomona College in the California Claremont system. A university engages in research that creates new knowledge about our world. In addition to the bachelor's degree, universities grant higher degrees such as the Master of Arts (MA) or other master's-level degrees, as well as the doctorate (PhD).

The advantage of a small stand-alone liberal arts college is that it tends to have faculty members who are focused on teaching and not as heavily on research. They have more time to spend with students. Their tenure (permanent employment) is based on how well they teach more than on how many books or other academic publications they have produced, or how much funding they have brought to the college to finance their research interests. Classes may be smaller, and they are usually taught by full-time professors, rather than adjuncts (usually part-time non-staff instructors) or graduate students who are scholars and professors in training (more often found at research universities). While adjunct professors are often wonderful teachers, they may not have as much time to spend with students or as much knowledge of the college itself. Graduate students may be closer in age to undergraduates and so more understanding; however, while they may be knowledgeable and insightful about the program itself, they do not yet know as much about their subjects as seasoned full-time professors.

On the other hand, a research university is filled with resources and opportunities for students themselves to engage in research. Professors are at the top of their fields, there is a lot of energy at the school around scholarship, and expectations are high for faculty to produce publications as evidence of the new knowledge they have generated. Though large, these universities are exciting places to be. Students can have the best of both worlds if the school manages the undergraduate experience so that it is a more intimate one.

Info: Higher Education Degrees

Here is a list of the type of degrees or programs you may consider:

- A **certificate program** does not grant a degree and does not have the rigorous expectations of a degree granting program, but certifies that the student has taken coursework leading to a level of proficiency in a stated area—such as a CASAC, a certificate in alcoholism and substance abuse counseling.

- An **Associate's** degree (AA, Associate in Arts) requires two years of work for a degree in general studies (such as an associate in liberal arts), or one specialized in a profession, such as an AS (Associate of Science, in community health), or an AAS (Associate in Applied Sciences, in early childhood education, nursing, or recreation therapy).

- The **Bachelor's** degree commonly requires four years of study or the equivalent in credits. It may be a BA (Bachelor of Arts) or a BS (Bachelor of Science), depending on the concentration and offerings of the college.

- The **Master's** degree (MA) is a graduate degree earned after a BA and may require a year or two, or the equivalent in credits, depending on the program. It is a specialization or concentration in a particular subject or field. For example, an MBA is a Master in Business Administration, an MFA a Master of Fine Arts, an MSW a degree in social work, and an MPA a Master of Public Administration. One can also earn an MA in history or biology or math. An MA is usually required before, or as part of, earning the doctorate, with variations from school to school.

- A **Doctorate** is considered a "terminal degree," meaning it is the highest degree you can earn in the field of your choosing. A doctoral degree can be general, a Doctor of Philosophy (PhD), or specific, such as a Juris Doctor or JD (law degree), an MD, Doctor of Medicine, or an EdD, Doctor of Education. (Note that these abbreviations all have their origins in Latin; for example, *Juris Doctor* means Doctor of Law.)

Underchallenged

You were bored and didn't achieve at the level people believed you could with the right effort. Did teachers and others tell you all the time how smart you were (even when they said you weren't fulfilling your potential)? Were you among those who found school easy? Maybe you did not like school because it was not challenging enough. Well, challenges will come at college.

If you were underachieving, you may have burned some bridges. Your grades may not match your Scholastic Aptitude Test (SAT) scores. The SAT sometimes captures your potential more accurately, and high SAT scores (650+ for each section) may increase your college options. On the other hand, if you didn't get good grades and are among those who do not test well, your choices are limited even further. All is not lost, however. You may have to start out at a less prestigious college, then consider transferring once you show what you're made of by embracing the full challenges of college life.

Some schools may not be top tier, but they offer greater enrichment along the way, in the form of honors programs and special research opportunities. So you may land in a school that offers you support and the chance to excel. You may become the big fish in the small pond. Your chances of finishing in the top of your class may be increased, which in turn increases your options later on.

If your experience matches that described here, you may consider a liberal arts college or be attracted to some of the other options in the next sections. Like the student adrift, you may want to take some time off.

A Story: Tom

Tom was in high school when his dad was diagnosed with cancer. Several painful years passed while he watched his beloved father gradually pass away. Tom was a talented student at an excellent high school, but he was devastated. He drifted through the years. Then he was pulled up short when he realized, at the end of his junior year, that his grades were now going to be a problem as he applied to colleges. He set his sights on a different place than some of his classmates and began to explore small state colleges. He found one not too far from home, so that he would be able to visit his mother on weekends. Recognizing his potential, the school pointed him toward an honors program, provided he did well in his first year. Tom began to thrive again and is now enrolling in graduate school, with an eye on a doctorate, made possible because he was a top student in the honors program at his college.

Don't Need College (Now)

Your path may lead to being an artist or creative person who has to follow a passion unbound by pedagogy. You are a dancer, an artist, a filmmaker, a carpenter, a fashion designer. You just want to get to work. You don't want to wait to do what you love and don't see that college is going to help you. Perhaps you'll take some courses along the way, but you don't need college full-time, at least not now. A chance to work with a great designer, to study art in Europe, to make a film on a current event—these are all reasons to postpone college. Part of your challenge may be to persuade parents or family that you want to postpone this milestone activity.

A woman I admire greatly danced for George Balanchine throughout her young adult years and didn't have a chance to go to college until she was well into her thirties. She then went on to earn a doctorate and taught college English for the next thirty years.

Another student at NYU had an opportunity to dance with the New York City Ballet that would not wait until after she finished college. In her second year with the company, however, she suffered an injury and decided to head off to school, where she completed a degree in economics.

So if you are creative, you may want or even need to defer college—but don't take it off the agenda. Ninety percent of the time, more education will enhance your options. You may refine your craft in practical courses, such as an art studio class. You may learn to teach your skill, or learn skills that enable you to make a living doing what you love. Film students can take business courses; playwrights can learn to teach writing to sustain themselves. There are many schools, such as the Illinois Institute of Art and Ohio's Columbus College of Art and Design, that specialize in creative pursuits ranging from animation to fine arts, film, dance, and theater. Some offer combination degrees in art therapy, art restoration, or fashion retailing. There may be scholarships or internships that relate to your passion as well—a summer theater program seeking college students, for example. College-related experiences and alumni contacts may actually better build a résumé in a competitive creative arena than going it alone.

Returning Student

You are older than the traditional student and have family and home responsibilities to manage. Perhaps you felt long ago that you weren't ready for or did not need college, or now you're dead-ended in a career and need to develop new skills.

More than likely you are in the category of adult learner. You're over twenty-five. Your time is precious. At some point you realize that to progress in your work or to move to a more lucrative field, you need a college degree or more training in a specific area. You are part of a large and growing group for whom increasing resources are available.

It has been noted that returning students are more focused, work harder, and often do better, so many colleges are coming to value them greatly.

There are now lots of online options like the University of Phoenix or hybrid institutions like DeVry and Kaplan that are targeted to your needs. Many traditional universities are offering some mix of online and onsite courses. Public universities and schools in urban centers are often more attuned to the needs of the adult learner. Community colleges again are excellent choices, as they are more flexible in scheduling and can offer courses specific to certain career goals. Some give credit for life experience or allow you to use your work as part of your learning experience.

Many schools offer courses in the evenings or on weekends, or special programs designed for the working student. It is challenging, for instance, when your curriculum requires lab time, but lab facilities and faculty are available only during your work hours. But some schools now even offer labs on the weekends. While it requires some adjustment to be among much younger students, the perseverance and hard work will pay off in excellence.

Hands-On Learner

You learn best by doing and are practical in your interests. In high school, did you prefer the courses that demanded the most practical approaches or allowed you to work with your hands? Does action take precedence over reading or researching in the library?

There are students, and you may be one, for whom a traditional college is not the right choice.

There are colleges, sometimes classified as technical colleges, that are clearly vocational in their focus and teach hands-on skills that can be used right away in defined workplaces. These teach specific skills, for example, in mechanics or computer repair. They focus on the technical skills required for particular careers, though also providing other related and important subject areas, such as business management, communications, or quantitative skills courses.

In this category are for-profit schools, such as DeVry (with more than ninety sites nationally), which offers a range of vocationally centered college degrees. Metropolitan College of New York, a small private school, has a history of training students for business and human services careers. A public institution such as the City University of New York's John Jay College specializes in criminal justice matters. The large private University of Phoenix has campuses all over the country and offers a wide range of vocationally oriented degrees well suited to the student who is already in the workplace. Technical schools offering degrees in specific fields include the acclaimed Cordon Bleu Schools, which teach cooking and restaurant management and are found in many cities. These types of institutions, which offer evening, weekend, or online classes, may also appeal to the mature, returning, or working student. Such schools may be advertised on television, public transportation, radio, and certainly on the Web.

Those mentioned previously all have long histories. They are accredited by their regional accrediting organizations and also usually by professional associations. *But make sure that any school you attend is accredited by the major associations.* Also be sure that it is approved by your state board of education or board of regents. In the case of some for-profit schools, check their standing for ethical business practices with the Better Business Bureau, and validate, especially, the truth of their job placement and salary statistics. These for-profits may not offer financial aid options comparable to other types of schools, so you want to be sure your money is well spent.

Info: Accreditation

There are regional bodies that review colleges and universities on a variety of measures, including governance, financial stability, and most important, academic outcomes. They give "accreditation" to those schools that meet their standards. According to the U.S. Department of Education, the goal of accreditation is to "assure that institutions of higher education meet acceptable standards of quality." Federal financial aid is given only to schools that meet those standards. A list of accredited colleges meeting federal standards can be found at **http://ope.edu.gov/accreditation/**.

Adrift

You are not yet sure if college is right for you, or more important, if you are ready for college. Do you feel pushed to go to school, but not quite focused enough to settle down to a course of study? Are you feeling that you don't have a sense of purpose? Are you looking for a purpose?

While everyone else seems so assured about college goals, you want to experience more before you take the plunge. You may have been derailed by a traumatic event. Your grades may not be great, and you wonder if you are worthy of the investment. Or you may just feel wobbly about your situation. If so, you may be the kind of student who should take a year off before starting college.

Perhaps you should work for a year while you find your focus. Or you may want to engage in some kind of service here in this country or abroad, to test your capacity for independence and assert yourself.

Taking a year off between high school and college is no longer frowned upon by admissions committees—*if* the student uses the time well and can show increased maturity and clarity of focus as a result. Keeping a journal during this time can be valuable. As a member of an admissions committee, I remember the discussion about a student who did volunteer work in Mexico for a year and wrote poetry about the experience—and how impressed we were. Volunteer service, unique travel, or even a job that takes you clearly out of your comfort zone, can be just what you need to clarify your purpose and how college can help you fulfill it. You can find resource information through the Corporation for National and Community Service at **www.nationalservice.org**.

There is no question that students who are clear about why they're in school—even if they haven't yet decided on a major or career choice—do better than those who, because they are drifting along, are more susceptible to distractions that can be damaging. If you are feeling adrift, it is better to postpone your investment until your own dedication assures the return you want.

Less-than-Dazzling Record

Are your grades not what they should be? Maybe you had a rough patch along the way. Perhaps your friends did not value education and you let yourself be pulled along with them, to the detriment of your grades. Maybe your grades are uneven—you are great in English, but terrible at math, and it shows in your grade point average (GPA) and college test scores such as the SAT or ACT. But you know you want to go to college.

For whatever reason, your grades are below the threshold that most private and many state institutions seek. Or you may have good grades, but come from a high school that has not prepared you well to compete with students who have more rigorous training. Or your SAT scores are not great, though your grades are respectable. Any combination of these circumstances may preclude your being at the top of the list for many schools. But that does not mean you cannot go to college.

If there is a good reason for your slide in grades or your test-taking problems, address it in your college application. If you had to deal with the death of a parent, a divorce, or other crisis, say so. If you have learning disabilities that require special attention, then be able to show that you have been tested for them. (Such test results may be useful later in college as well.) Your college essay is where some of this can be revealed, and while the information may not fully overcome the numbers, it may help keep you in the running. How well your high school teachers express their support of your capacities in their recommendations can help, too.

If you are a returning veteran or an ex-offender whose special circumstances and needs must be considered, there are programs all over the country to help you make the transition to college—you should look for the ones in your area. Some programs are even located on college campuses. There are many examples of successful individuals who have overcome the trauma of battle or the stigma of a criminal record. I have known both kinds of students and admire the strength they have brought to surmounting tough circumstances.

Perhaps you did not even finish high school. You wanted or needed to get work to support your family. Or you fell into the attitude that school was not cool and you did not need it. Then you discovered that you were feeling passionate about a career area and would need a college degree to advance in the field, or that you couldn't even get a job related to the field without at least a high school diploma. Doors were closed to you—now you want to not only finish high school, but go on to college.

Your first step is to check into the **GED (General Equivalency Diploma)** programs, which are widely available. You can acquire one of these general education diplomas by passing a test to show that you have mastered high school equivalency requirements and skills. The GED is administered by the American Council of Education through departments of education in individual states. It can be taken only at official test centers across the country, not through any online process. According to **http://www.gedprograms.org**, "the test is a seven-hour exam which is broken down into five separate smaller tests based on subject area: math, social studies, science, language arts reading, and language arts writing. A student must pass each of the five tests. Most school districts do not require that all five exams be taken on the same day."

The majority of the exam consists of answering questions using a multiple-choice format. Each correct answer is worth one point. For each individual test, points are totaled and then converted to a standard score, which ranges from 200 to 800. Candidates need a standard score of at least 410 on each of the GED tests in order to pass and an overall score of 450 as an average for the five-test GED battery.

In Part II of the Language Arts: Writing section, students are required to write an essay that must contain at least five paragraphs supporting a thesis statement assigned by the test itself. Most test takers do not pass on the first try. Only three out of every ten students pass all five exams on their first try.

Often community colleges and local work-training programs offer GED preparation. At some colleges, passing can mean automatic enrollment. In some states prisons also offer GED programs for their inmates so they can be more employable upon release.

A Story: Maurice

Maurice was at Sing-Sing Prison in New York State, with a record of violent gang activity and substance abuse. A counselor and correctional officer recognized his intelligence and encouraged him to get his GED and turn his life around. When released, Maurice earned a college degree and then a master's degree. He is now working toward a PhD in social work and is a counselor to other men in similar circumstances. He is highly regarded in his field and is a role model not only to other students, but to his own children.

The Community College Option

If you face any of these circumstances, an excellent option for you might be a community college. There are over twelve hundred in the United States, and they are a good value. They are typically publicly funded, meaning subsidized, so the expense is reasonable. They take students from local high schools and communities and know intimately the strengths and weaknesses of local school systems. They offer remediation where needed, often in math or language skills, and are more forgiving of students not familiar with college culture.

The White House has recognized the importance of community colleges and is investing heavily in them. These schools are often especially attuned to the first-generation college student and can be welcoming environments for the nontraditional student. There is, as well, a more vocational focus. The faculty, like that of the best small liberal arts colleges, is dedicated to teaching. You can catch up in skills and show your good attributes. If you do well and are dedicated, you may go on to a four-year college or move up from an associate's to a bachelor's degree track. You may surprise yourself and find that you have talents and interests you never expected.

There are rewards for outstanding performance at a community college. The Jack Kent Cooke Foundation gives money to top students who are viable candidates for top four-year colleges. Those schools, seeking diversity, may draw on the more urban or diverse population of a community college. So a student from Kingsborough Community College in Brooklyn or California's Canada Community College may end up at the prestigious Smith College or Stanford University for junior and senior years.

The Online Option

Also look at online courses. Note that employers still don't ascribe as much value to online degrees, but if you can do a mix of online and classroom courses at a fully accredited college or university, then you might more easily manage the time-life balance that can be required of an older or returning student. Note that online courses have become much more than just videos of lectures and are often fully interactive and quite demanding. Facebook is a model for them—a community of students interacting with an instructor and one another. Look for programs with a strong reputation (perhaps using adjunct faculty from local businesses), and expect to work hard. Again, you want to be sure the school has been accredited (approved) by the organizations that validate college quality. Check **http://www.yourdegree.com/**, which lists accredited online schools.

Courses taught by famous or highly popular faculty at prominent institutions are also now available online for free. These cannot take the place of your existing courses or requirements, but they can be useful supplements or preparation when you want to pursue a subject through a different voice than the ones your college offers. A popular site is the Opencourseware consortium (**www.ocwconsortium.org**), but you can find courses on iTunes and YouTube as well.

The Easing-In Option

It is useful sometimes to consider taking on higher education in chunks. You might get through a two-year program with your associate's degree to prove to yourself that you can do it, before you move up to the next level. If you plan to take this route, strategize to be sure you are building the proper credits for a move to a four-year school. On the graduate level, you can earn a master's degree before you commit to a doctorate. Take it step by step and it is less intimidating.

Taking time off, as suggested to the adrift student, can be a good strategy too, but it should include taking courses at the college level to show you can do the work. Or use some of the time to prepare for and retake the SAT or ACT. Some of the schools advisable for the hands-on learner may also be appropriate for you to strengthen your academic skills and show a school that you are serious about getting your education.

Clear Career Path

You have always known what you want to be when you grow up. Have you always known you want to be a doctor, lawyer, executive, nurse, scientist, teacher...?

From the time your grandmother gave you a doctor's kit, you knew you would be an MD. Seeing Jack McCoy at work on *Law and Order* persuaded you that you wanted to be a lawyer. Your mother's illness showed you what special work nurses do. Every day of your school life has been leading to a specific goal, and you have not wavered in that pursuit.

All of these professions require a college degree. If you are clearly focused on and passionate about such a life path, then not only do you need college, but most likely you need one that will support that goal in particular. With that being said, while this book's discussion on courses and majors comes later, this caution comes now: *It is okay to change your mind.* And college may do that.

But if you have a career in mind, then in seeking a college, be sure to find one that is strong in your area of interest and provides support for the goal you want to pursue. The career office should have data on how many alumni go to medical or law schools, or land careers at investment banks or get MBAs, and on what schools they attend. Find out who prepares students for these outcomes. Pay attention to resources that will support your goals, rather than to majors, which do not correlate to careers (more on this later). Is there a prelaw club, a moot court program, a Model UN program, corporate internships? Larger campuses are more likely to be rich in these resources. Once at college, you will want to engage in the relevant programs the school offers and even become a leader in professionally affiliated clubs and programs.

Look at public or private universities—some may have these types of schools affiliated with them. Columbia has a school of education, Teacher's College; Hunter College, a School of Social Work; Stanford, a School of Journalism; Michigan, a School of Law; Morgan State University, a School of Business. The advantage here is that graduate students are available to consult about their programs, and alumni are easily accessible. (Note, however, that graduate programs do not always give special treatment to undergraduate applicants from the same institution.)

No Resources

You feel you can't afford to go to college. You want to go, but there is no money for school. No one in your family has attended college, so it seems too difficult and out of reach for you. You may have family obligations already and can't see how this can work for you.

Put these thoughts away! If you are dedicated and really want to go, the funds can generally be found. You may have to be both persistent and creative, but you can do it.

First, for U.S. citizens, there are federal funds available—usually in the form of Pell grants, student loans, work-study programs, deferred tuition programs (such as AmeriCorps), or outright scholarships tied to specific areas. Taking out credit union loans is a good strategy, if you need to borrow money. State funds vary by state—Wisconsin, for instance, offers the Wisconsin Tuition Grant Program (WTG). Private donors, clubs, and fraternal organizations also offer funds, and some may be available to those without green cards or who are not yet naturalized citizens. College scholarship funds can be merit-based or need-based, the latter requiring applicants to supply financial information, including a copy of your tax return. Some employers offer tuition support if the schooling relates to the job.

You may decide to work and take evening courses, paying as you go. This method takes longer and is more taxing, but colleges such as the University of Phoenix are geared to that approach. State and city public college systems are economical for local working students and are often truly stellar.

You need to shop for the schools that offer the best value for the money. *Princeton Review* and *U.S. News and World Report* feature lists of such schools around the country. The best place to start gathering information is the Department of Education, **http://federalstudentaid.ed.gov**. Or visit the site **www.finaid.org**, which will lead you to a wide array of financial sources. A useful new site, **http://www.studentaid.ed.gov**, lists resources and strategies for preparing for college.

Whatever you do, *do not* put tuition on a credit card. Go for a student loan. These loans do not become due until after you graduate, and they carry a far lower interest rate. You end up with less debt and more latitude in paying it off. In some cases, there is even loan forgiveness if you enter certain fields.

Just remember that your earning power is directly related to the amount of education you have. A college graduate earns 54 percent more than someone who does not graduate, and 74 percent more than someone with only a high school diploma. So the longer you put off getting a degree, the longer you may be trapped in a low-income position where you have little leverage.

THE PAYOFF!

Yes, college will help you find a job and prepare you for advancement, but there are other valuable benefits. Wherever you go to school, if you are in the place that's right for you, your life will be enhanced. You will know yourself better, have a better idea of your strengths and weaknesses, likes and dislikes, and goals. You will have a clearer conception of the world around you—the physical environment, the political arena, and the community, both local and global. You will see better how you fit into those domains. Finally, you will have learned new skills.

Newly learned skills might include the ability to manage your time more effectively, conduct research, solve and even anticipate complex problems, or connect with others with greater facility. Ideally you will have increased your skills in all these areas. While having a strong academic record will get you part of the way toward your goals, it is these other abilities that will serve you over the long term.

For each class you take, ask yourself if it has helped you see yourself better, helped you know more about the world, and whether you have learned a new skill. Add that up over the thirty-two or more courses you'll take in college, and you'll see that there's a great deal to gain indeed.

Info: If You're Not a Citizen

What if you are not a U.S. citizen? What are the implications for you with regard to attending college in the United States?

It is possible—you can go to college. You may enter on a student visa. For an F or M visa, you must have a residence in your country of origin to which you plan to return, and you must meet the following other requirements:

- Be enrolled in an academic educational program (see requirements below), a language e-training program, or a vocational program
- Be enrolled in a school approved by the U.S. Citizenship and Immigration Services (USCIS, formerly known as the INS)
- Be enrolled as a full-time student at the institution
- Be proficient in English or be enrolled in courses leading to English proficiency
- Have sufficient funds available for self-support during the entire proposed course of study

Schools can apply to allow non-citizens to enroll—most public and many private institutions have done so. You can also come on a J visa as part of an educational exchange program. It is wise to check the Immigration Services website sections relating to student visas at **www.uscis.gov**.

If you are living here without benefit of a green card, then the consequences may be significant: You are not eligible for any federal or government loans or financial aid that comes from tax dollars. Although you and perhaps most of your family live here, you are generally categorized as an "international student." This means that if your state or city has differing tuition rates for in- or out-of-state students, you have to pay the higher out-of-state rate. College is, then, likely to be expensive for you. Some schools have funds from private donors (not tax-levy funds) that they can use or that are designated for scholarships for students in your situation. Check with the financial aid office regarding availability of such funds at your school. If a college wants to recruit or retain you, they can work to do so, resources permitting.

There are other challenges you face as well. For example, you do not qualify for federally funded research, remedial, or pipeline-to-graduate-school programs because they are government sponsored. Privately funded foundation programs may offer more latitude, but there are fewer of them. Similarly, government-based internship programs typically limit participation to those with green cards or citizenship. Some professional schools that lead to government licensing (law and medicine) may discourage your enrollment, unless you are likely to be naturalized by the time you complete the graduate degree.

Postgraduate fellowships such as the Marshall and Fulbright grants are also restricted to those with citizenship. For the Rhodes, if you originate in a former British Commonwealth country, some countries' rules may allow you to apply from that country; others restrict Rhodes applicants to those enrolled in local schools. Be sure to read the rules carefully before doing the work of applying to any programs.

The rationale for these policies, which may seem harsh and unfair, is that funds derived from taxpayer dollars should be spent first on U.S. citizens. Seen in this light, and given the competition for such funds and programs, the policies may make more sense—but they do not make your life any easier. Talk to the offices at your school that have experience with these issues—an office for international students or special advisors or officials in financial aid. You are not the first person to bring them the problem, and they may offer strategies for helping you achieve your goals despite these barriers.

Chapter 2
FINANCING YOUR EDUCATION

Studies indicate that the reason many students drop out of college has to do with money. You took a job to pay for college, but it takes too much of your time, so you're not doing well. You didn't apply for aid and then lost the job you thought would pay for your schooling. You didn't budget well and fell short of what you need, or a crisis chewed up what you put away to pay for tuition. You threw away the letter with your bill or deleted the email telling you that you owed money. You dropped too many classes and lost your financial aid (dropping too many courses or signing up for too few can change your status to part-time, where you are not eligible for aid). Many of the lessons in this book help you deal with situations such as these.

Your college emphasizes that you are responsible for the funding of your education—indeed, you must pay attention to finances all the way through school and, certainly, beyond. You need to think about which school you attend in terms of finances and what your future life will be like so that you plan wisely and do not burden yourself unduly. Here, we will also point you toward the essential steps in the federal loan process and suggest additional sources for funds. A sample budget will help your planning. Throughout this book, we point out ways to be careful about handling your finances for school. The important thing to remember is that with creativity and perseverance you can finance your education!

ACCESSING FEDERAL FUNDS

First, *before* you sign up for school, be sure you have the funds in hand. They may be coming through your financial aid package that was included with your acceptance letter. Unless you have been told in writing that all your expenses are covered, there is some part of the bill that is yours to pay. (A rare and lucky few exceptional students, who combine academic excellence and need, are attractive candidates for scholarships.) Be sure you have done your planning and are prepared. You wouldn't normally go to the grocery store to buy ice cream without having your money in hand—college is no different.

The good news is that more federal funds are being made available to finance your education. The bad news is that getting access to that money and filling out the key federal form, the **FAFSA (Free Application for Federal Student Aid),** is a complex process. (Note that you are not eligible for government support if you are not a U.S. citizen.)

To be eligible for federal Pell grants, loans, or even campus-based aid, you must have filled out the FAFSA. In fact, it is a good idea to do so even if you are lucky enough not to need aid. This is problematic if your family is not filing tax returns, as the return for the previous year is required for financial aid applications and even for some government-sponsored scholarships that are predicated on proven need, as demonstrated by the return. Some public colleges will enroll you and even find private funding sources for you, but in most cases you have to be able and willing to submit the FAFSA form. If a crisis such as illness in the family or loss of a job occurs, you may need to appeal for support, which will require you to be in the system—even if right now you could pay the whole bill. It is best to work with the financial aid office—the advisors are trained to guide and counsel you on how to get aid.

It is often the students who most need financial aid or guidance to find ways to pay for college who are shy or embarrassed to do so. Students who do not come from families where others have attended college or where there is not a lot of money may have the least information about the process and available resources. If this is you, then you need to be aware that you are more likely to have higher debt because of lack of information—so always ask. One student was about to transfer from a low-cost local public institution to a high-cost out-of-state school because he was at risk of losing a scholarship. He talked to a dean and found that he could get aid to reduce his job hours, change majors, and improve his record. He thus saved his scholarship and no longer needed to transfer, which would have cost him more in the long run in loans he did not actually need.

Most of us hesitate to talk about money, yet it is an area that has huge significance. Learning about financial resources can not only save you lots of money, and perhaps save your education, but doing so becomes an essential part of that education.

Getting Your FAFSA PIN

There is a process to getting financial aid. It can seem complex at first but it is essential.

The application process for financial aid is free. The application you will use is called the Free Application for Federal Student Aid (FAFSA). Go to the **www.fafsa.ed.gov** site (if you prefer, you can complete your FAFSA in Spanish).

It is strongly suggested that you complete your FAFSA online. Before you begin that process, obtain a federal Personal Identification Number (PIN).

- Apply at the Department of Education's PIN site, **www.pin.ed.gov**.
- Select "PIN Request and Information," followed by "Apply for PIN."

The PIN serves as your identifier to let you access your personal information in various U.S. Department of Education systems. It's like the PIN you get from your bank that enables you to access your account. Because your PIN serves as your electronic signature, you should not give it to anyone. It should take seven to ten days to receive your PIN, but signing up to get it by email reduces the turnaround time to three days. Once you are assigned a PIN, you can go online and change it to something easy for you to remember. Once you have a PIN, you can begin!

- Go to the **www.fafsa.ed.gov** site, and be ready to provide all the information required.

Required Documents

You'll need records of income earned in the year before you start school. These include the following:

- your W-2 Forms and other records of money earned
- your (and your spouse's, if you're married) Federal Income Tax Return—IRS Form 1040, 1040A, 1040EZ, 1040Telefile, foreign tax return, or tax return for Puerto Rico, Guam, American Samoa, U.S. Virgin Islands, Marshall Islands, or the Federated States of Micronesia
- your untaxed income records—Social Security, Temporary Assistance to Needy Families, welfare, veterans benefits
- your bank statements
- your Social Security number, alien registration number, and/or driver's license number
- your business, investment, and mortgage information; business and farm records; stocks, bonds, and other information about property you or your parents may own
- your parents' financial information. Even if your parents are not planning to contribute to your tuition, if you are classified as a dependent student, their income information is required for completing the FAFSA. You are considered dependent if you are unmarried, under twenty-four years of age, have no financial dependents, and are not an orphan, a ward of the court, or a veteran of the U.S. armed forces.
- your parents' previous-year federal income tax return, as well as their records of all the items listed above (i.e., W-2 forms, untaxed income records, bank statements, etc.)

Financial Aid and Independent Status

For students who are returning to school as adults or who are fully independent of parental financial support, your financial aid picture may be different. Your income, which may be less or even more than your parents', will be the only one on which your financial aid need is based. But proving that you are indeed independent is a challenge. You will qualify if you

- are married, over twenty-four, a veteran or in the military, a ward of the state, or demonstrably homeless
- possess evidence of your status.

Otherwise you really must have both parents—whether together or not—submit information for the FAFSA. When difficult situations exist, such as an acrimonious divorce, a missing parent, or a parent who is not maintaining his or her responsibilities, discuss it with the financial aid officers of the college. But just wanting to be independent will not do, unless you meet the above criteria.

Claiming independent status may not serve you well. For example, a recent study by the College Board Policy and Advocacy Center indicates that students who are listed as independent graduate with more college debt than students still dependent on parents or other guardians for some of their support. This is especially true for students who are low income. Again, your advisor and financial aid office can help.

FINDING FUNDS

Look at sources of funds that you may not have thought of. **Credit unions** are a good one, and they are anxious to make student loans. Unlike banks, which are corporations, these are collectives owned by the members, and they are often more reliable, customer friendly, and stable.

If your choice is between going to school with a loan or not getting an education, then the loan, managed responsibly, is the better choice. If you wait to attend school or try to extend your time in college by attempting to earn the tuition each term, you are deferring higher wages.

A new service, worth exploring, has emerged—SafeStart (**http://student loan.boomja.com/SafeStart-94999.html**), which is owned by the Bridgespan company. SafeStart is designed to make the risk of taking college loans more manageable.

College debt is a necessary evil, but an evil nonetheless. A program such as SafeStart, which has been written up in both *USA Today* and the *New York Times,* is meant to take some of the pain out of the loan payment issue. Another resource is **www.edvisors.com**, which focuses on online education and financial resources.

If you have secured financial aid through loans, you have to think about paying them back—in fact, you should think about that early on. For example, if you know that you are going into a field like social work (a much-needed but not high-paying field), you will want to align the level of your loans to what you may realistically earn. This may mean going to a school where you will not need as much in loan debt. If you have choices about colleges, think about what the long-term picture will be. On the other hand, there is good news that for those starting college after July 2010, the burden of college loans has been eased somewhat.

On March 30, 2010, President Obama signed the Student Aid Fiscal Responsibility Act (SAFRA) into law. This landmark piece of reform legislation is intended to reboot the floundering student loan industry by redirecting all new federal loans through the Department of Education and enhancing pro–financial aid initiatives, while eliminating other controversial elements of past practices. Many of its features took effect in July 2010. According to **FinancialAidNews.com** (April 12, 2010),

> *...After July, any new loans you take out will all be through FDLP [a federal government program], at a lower interest rate, and with a more flexible array of repayment plans.*
>
> *Income Based Repayment (IBR) is one of the best things to ever happen to student borrowers. Essentially, if your total payments for*

the year equate to higher than 15% of your annual income, you are eligible to have your payments drastically lowered. For instance, under IBR, an income of $15,000 (for a household size of one) or less would make your monthly payment on all federal student loans $0. That's right, no payments at all. As the household size increases, the maximum income level to qualify for IBR rises as well. The Student Loan Network has assembled a great chart on Income Based Repayment information that presents the data in an easy-to-digest format.

The benefits of IBR don't stop there. In addition to potentially having your monthly payments significantly reduced (or eliminated), you actually can have the loans forgiven if they are in good standing and all payments are made on time for a certain amount of time. In some cases, federal student loans will be forgiven after 10 years (this is based on a "hot fields" list of desirable professions) and 25 years for everyone else. If you are wondering what is exactly meant by loan "forgiveness," it means your loan gets cancelled, and you no longer have to pay it back or have the debt sitting on your credit history.

The ideal is to avoid loans if you can, or to keep the portion of aid to be repaid as low as possible. This is where private scholarships are very important and your high school successes can pay off.

A Cautionary Tale: Erica's Bad Decisions

Erica was financing college through a Pell grant and a small scholarship, but needed to come up with $2,000 more before registration. She was counting on a loan from a friend, who at the last minute couldn't come through. Then she thought about using her credit card, but her credit limit was too low. She had already signed up for classes, some of which were difficult to get into, and when she couldn't pay in time, she was dropped from them. Erica ended up having to postpone her plans for school for another semester.

Lessons learned: Have money in hand at the time you need it. Beware of credit cards, which will cost you more than a student loan. And don't use your friends, which can cost you your friendships. Planning ahead will make it possible to slowly build some savings. Taking a student loan will be less expensive over the long term than credit card debt.

Use the Web and libraries to also seek out private scholarships. There are many geared to particular populations. I once ran across one for residents of Hampden County, Massachusetts. And we actually found a student at our college who was from there! The Broadway show *In the Heights* has created a scholarship fund called Graduate to New Heights. There are also scholarships for women over thirty or for veterans or people of Polish descent. Do your homework and you may find a scholarship fit just for you.

That said, also beware of websites or consultants who charge large fees for scholarship searches that you can actually conduct yourself with some time and effort. The best source to search by yourself is **www.finaid.org**. And it is free!

When doing your research, remember too that there is a difference between what can be called the "sticker price" for college and the actual price. The published tuition is not what the majority of students actually pay. Deduct from that figure any scholarships, federal or state financial aid, or work-study funds, and what you have is the actual price. Thus the "sticker price" per year can go from $40,000 down to a few thousand dollars in the case of a private college. Or in the case of public colleges, it can go from a sticker price of a few thousand to zero. This is why it is so important to do the FAFSA and work with the financial aid office. While sticker prices have gone up in some cases, actual or net prices have held steady or gone down—and new legislation may make that more true.

Note that recent changes in federal rules under the new SAFRA legislation can work to your benefit. For example, there is more **loan forgiveness** for work in certain fields or geographic locations. A long list of loan forgiveness criteria can range from public service to a school's fraudulent practices. Go to: **http://www.studentloannetwork.com/repayment/forgiveness.php.** There will be more government changes to come. Your financial aid office will be tracking them and will be prepared to help you take advantage of them. It is always beneficial to follow current events, so you can ask intelligent, timely questions.

BEING FINANCIALLY SAVVY FOR LIFE

Paying for college is a planning process and a discipline you will use all your life. Learning about money and your money style will be of use forever. You have to pay attention to finances all the way through school and, certainly, beyond. Now is a good time, because of tuition demands, for you to really look at your spending patterns. You want to graduate with as little debt as possible. Entry-level jobs do not usually pay stellar salaries, and you will need to adjust to new living expenses. You may want to go to graduate school, which will entail more debt, though it will increase your earning power considerably.

While in school, avoid credit cards, or use debit and prepaid cards, so you don't build up dangerous balances—these will result in interest payments that weigh you down for a lifetime. Some helpful books and materials on financial planning include

- **http://financialplan.about.com/cs/college/a/MoneyCollege.htm**
- Stacey Tisdale's excellent book, *The True Cost of Happiness*, which helps you plan with an understanding of your personal money style.

One of the great things about college is that so much is free. I knew a student who was aware of every free event going on around town. Your tuition costs cover a health club or gym access, some level of medical care, food at events, entertainment, tutoring, computer access, and so much more. You also get student discounts on museum entry and other cultural activities. And campuses are usually surrounded by low-cost restaurants catering to student-size appetites and budgets.

Financing Your Education: Reaching Your Goal

As part of learning about your financial style and beginning to think practically about your finances, here are tools and a budget that you can use to see where and how you spend and how you can make the adjustments needed to pay for your education.

(Prepared by Lolita A. Wood-Hill
Hunter College of The City University of New York)

Prepare for the Cost of School
College is expensive, and lenders look at creditworthiness!

- Talk with your family. Find out if and how much they can help.
- Look for scholarships through private, government, and school sources.
- Use credit cards sparingly.
- Check your credit history.
- Pay off all consumer debt.
- Get a roommate or a job or both.
- Maintain a budget.
- Budget for

1. Application fees (can mount to $1,000+ if not waived and you apply to several schools)
2. Clothing for interviews
3. Travel to interviews—air, ground, lodging, food
4. Moving expenses

Credit Cards, or How to Bankrupt Your Future
What are you actually paying?

An example:
- Balance: $1,000
  APR: 18 percent

- Monthly minimum payment: $20
- Finance charge: $1,396
- Total paid: $2,396
- Months to repay: 151 (twelve and a half years)

Paying for Your Education
Scholarships
- National Hispanic Scholarship Fund
- Gates Millennium Scholarships
- Institutional Scholarships
- Union Scholarships
- Incentive Scholarships
- Service-Obligated Scholarships

Loans (subsidized and unsubsidized)
- Corporations/Employers/Banks
- Federal/State Funding
- Community
- Private Organizations
- Family

Applying for aid
- What is the institution's philosophy of financial aid?
- What grants and loans are available to meet your needs?
- Can you meet your full needs using those resources?
- Will your parents be expected to provide financial information?
- Do you have any options if they refuse?
- What are the application deadlines?

What should you know about the loans you are offered?
- Loan amount offered and maximum loan available

- Cosigner requirements, if any
- Interest rate
- Impact on your credit history
- Availability of alternatives
- Repayment terms/grace period
- Deferment options

Who is responsible?

You are!

- Keep records of all information: amount, lender, repayment schedule, interest rate.
- The lender may sell your loan to another company. You are still responsible.
- Inform all lenders of any address or other contact information changes.

What impact will loans have on me after school?

- Disposable income will be reduced.
- If you have difficulty paying loans, ask lender about forbearance.
- If you default, your professional practice, personal financial life, and taxes are adversely affected.
- Do not ignore your obligation to repay loans!

How do you get organized?

- Buy a file cabinet.
- Make a file for each loan or grant that you receive.
- Weed out dated material on a regular basis.
- Make and stick to a budget.

Household Budget Items

Basics

- Mortgage payment or rent
- Taxes
- Insurance
- Groceries
- Electric/gas
- Water
- Garbage pickup
- Cleaning supplies
- Laundry
- Dry cleaning
- Home maintenance/improvement projects
- Towels, linens, etc.
- Clothing

Must have—or not!

Transportation

- Public transportation
- Car payments
- Insurance
- Gas
- Routine maintenance/repairs
- Air travel
- Rental cars

Entertainment

- Cable TV or satellite service
- Internet access
- Dining out

- Bars, clubs, etc.
- Sporting events
- Concerts
- Parties
- Lessons

What are you spending all this money on?

Communications
- Telephone
- Cellular phone and services

Health/Beauty
- Haircuts, hair salon
- Makeup
- Medical, dental, vision
- Weight loss, diet products
- Nutritional supplements

...and More
- Credit card payments
- Other loan payments
- Child care
- Items for children/elderly
- Allowances for children
- Books, magazines, music, etc.
- Investments
- Vacations
- Spending money
- Donations to church or charity
- Gifts (holidays, birthdays, anniversaries, etc.)
- Emergency fund

- Fast food
- Coffee, soft drinks, cigarettes, etc.
- Alcoholic beverages

Chapter 3
GET GOING:
THE PROCESSES

GETTING STARTED

While most colleges do pretty much the same things, no two campuses do things the same way. This is especially important to remember if you're a transfer student or returning to college after a long hiatus. The rules change from campus to campus, and over time even on the same campus.

The first information source to hold close is the **college catalog**. It actually represents the legal contract between you and the school. And it contains an important bit of language, which notes that the rules can be changed at any time. They don't change very often, though, and during your time as a student you should plan to abide by the catalog that is in effect the day you enroll, unless a new catalog is released. The catalog is now usually found on the college's website as well, and that version may be the most current. But keep the hard copy too.

Refer to it whenever you have questions, such as how to challenge a grade, what grades mean, or what happens if you're caught cheating or drinking on campus. If you fall afoul of the rules, the first thing school authorities will point to is the catalog, and someone will say to you, "But didn't you read?" Legally, you are expected to know what it contains. So become familiar with it, and keep it handy.

Another legal point involves your **email account**, which colleges now usually provide for students as the means of communication with you. To consider a worst-case scenario: if you have not paid your bill and you are about to be thrown out, you will likely receive an email as a letter with this news. (But do not toss out letters from your college—open them and pay attention.) If you ignore such emails, the college can still claim legitimately that you were notified—they have done what is required to reach you.

Why so harsh? In college, students' world begins to change as expectations rise that they are on the way to becoming responsible adults in society. Whereas in high school and at home someone has been telling you where to go, what to do, how to do it, and when, in college you are considered a more responsible, self-reliant person. Even students who have jobs and families, who know they have to pay their bills and taxes on time, sometimes think they can pay their tuition late. Or they think that the college will take care of them, the way someone did in high school if they don't abide by college rules or deadlines.

Being self-reliant does not mean that you do not seek help when you need it—quite the contrary! Seeking help is a sign of maturity. Asking questions and getting guidance is what self-reliant individuals do. They know where to go to get the answers they need.

A Cautionary Tale:
Susan and Her Missing Courses

Susan went to college and fell in love. She got married, got pregnant, and dropped out to take care of her baby.

When her daughter started first grade, Susan realized that she really wanted to go back to school. She reapplied and was re-accepted. In registering for her classes she referred to the old catalog that she had at home and followed the rules about core requirements.

She was doing very well and getting close to graduation when the computer system informed her that she had an unfulfilled requirement.

She was sure she had taken the course, but when she checked with her advisor she found out that in the time she'd been away from school the rules had changed. The new rules were listed in the current catalog, not the one she had at home. Had she not dropped out of school, but continued with few classes even over a long period, the old rules would have applied. As a **readmitted** student, however, she was subject to the new rules, and she had to take courses that had been added as requirements for graduation—which she could have done earlier in a timely way. Now she ended up having to pay for two classes during the summer and getting her degree later.

Lessons learned: *Always review the most current catalog. Be sure your advisors have approved your course plan in writing, in the event they make an error. Keep all documentation.*

Among the things that students stumble over is just getting started—finding classes and becoming a fully matriculated college student. Here are the processes you need to be aware of, and wary of, and how you learn about them for your college.

REGISTRATION

This term covers a whole host of processes that take place from the time you are accepted into school through course selection and advisement, paying your bill, and actually enrolling in the classes you have been approved to take. Registration is not a single step, though many schools designate a day of the week when all aspects of the process can be taken care of and coordinated or have a single office where these steps are handled. The players involved include an advisor and the offices of the registrar, bursar, and financial aid. Let's hope your college has a clear Web-based explanation and process for this key activity. If not, it will certainly be covered at first-year or transfer orientation.

First you want to be sure you are **matriculated**. This means you have been accepted or admitted into the school or program to which you applied. This process begins in the **admissions office**. Once you have applied, filled out all required paperwork, submitted personal statements or essays, recommendations, test scores, and transcripts, you will get a formal letter saying that you have or have not been accepted into the school. If you are accepted as a full- or part-time student moving toward completion of a degree or certificate, you are matriculated.

If you're not accepted as a matriculated student you may have other options, ranging from applying to other schools or taking courses at the school of your choice as a **non-matriculated** student. You are considered non-matriculated if you're taking courses "à la carte," with no program requirements toward a degree (and probably less access to resources). You could also be put on a waiting list for admission, but it is wise to have a backup plan, as wait lists are not guarantees of acceptance.

When you are matriculated, there are specific times and dates set aside for registration, usually depending on your year. Freshmen get special consideration—special arrangements may allow you to register ahead of the pack or during orientation. There is more support and guidance then, and you should take advantage of it. Seniors get priority treatment because they are working toward graduating and may need to get into popular courses. That leaves sophomores and juniors having to scramble a bit more. Again, it is really important to read all messages about registration dates and times and to know the **school calendar**. Make notes in your own planner or PDA. Popular classes fill up quickly, and you want to be first in line for them.

Class sizes are determined by various factors, including room size (as set by the fire department), room availability, or the nature of the course—a lecture for up to hundreds of students or a seminar focusing on discussion for a small group. Demand is also created by students' need to fulfill certain requirements in a particular time frame, such as biology for premed students being a prerequisite for other required premed classes. Some classes requiring labs for the practical application of lectures and readings may have limited physical space—which limits the numbers in the corresponding lecture. So when classes are closed out because they are fully enrolled, easily making adjustments is usually beyond anyone's control.

If you don't get into a class you need or desire at registration, this is not the time to panic.

Note that during registration, because students drop classes, courses that may have been closed out one day may open up the next. It is wise to stay on top of the process if there is a particular course you want or need, but are having trouble getting into. Timing can make all the difference. In some schools there may be a wait list managed either by the registrar or the faculty members concerned. Inquire about this, but do it nicely.

Advisors

Your next step should be meeting with an advisor to see that you're taking the right courses for your grade level and to fulfill requirements, and to be sure you are not taking too many or too few classes. If you have a low grade point average, for example, the school won't generally allow you to take more than a certain number of credits, so that you can focus on doing well in a reasonable number of classes.

As a transfer student, you want to be sure of which courses can be transferred from your previous school. This can sometimes take extra effort. There may be a particular office or transfer student advisor to help with this process. Be sure to save old syllabi or course descriptions for courses whose credits you hope to transfer. In some cases colleges have understandings with other schools called **articulation agreements**, which allow for automatic transfer of credits from one like or related school to another. Such decisions are made by faculty or with faculty input, not by admissions officers or registrars.

There are various kinds of advisors. In your first year or two it is the job of someone from an advising center, dean's office, or office of student affairs to guide you. This advisor is trained not only in the rules of the school and curriculum, but also to help support you in many ways, including during personal crises—he or she is your ally. In some cases the advising center may be coupled with the registrar's, bursar's, and financial aid offices, for a one-stop shopping experience. For example, if your advisor suggests that you add a class, you might, in the same space, make adjustments to your program and your bill through the registrar and bursar. It goes without saying that you should always pay attention to your advisors; as noted earlier, never ignore notices, letters, or emails from any of the offices mentioned.

A Story: Joe

Joe was a bright young man who was doing well academically and was involved in many campus activities. When the deans were considering nominations for prestigious scholarships, his name came up, and he got to know his dean well. When he had a crisis in one of his classes, she was able to provide support to get him through the difficulty successfully. Joe continued doing well and went on to do graduate work at Oxford in England. He is still close to that dean today, as she continues to play a role in his life and work.

In some schools you cannot go online to register unless your advisor has signed off on your plan—at least in your first year or two. You may be able to make changes in your program without your advisor's knowledge in some cases, but that may become a problem later if the changes don't serve you well. If problems later crop up, the advisor can point to the advice given to you (which is often on record in a file or online), and you will have to take responsibility for your contrary independent decision. If you are unsure, always ask.

Once you have declared your major, most likely a faculty member in your major department will guide you through the department's rules. Faculty members may not be as savvy about all the college's rules and requirements, however, so keep in touch with your original advisor too. Remember, the more college officials who know you and know your strengths and challenges, the better they can serve you in achieving your goals. Your faculty advisor, for example, may be the one to nominate you for honors or scholarships. When calls go out asking for students to recommend for various programs and opportunities, the ones who come to mind are those whom officials know. Hiding out does not get you anywhere.

The Bursar

I remember having to stand in very long lines for a very long time to submit my course plan, get the bill, and pay the bill. Most schools now have online processes that are much easier. But in either case, the important thing to know is that registering for a class, getting billed for it, and paying the bill are all connected activities. You are not actually registered unless your bill is paid. That is where the office of the bursar (think of the term *disbursement*) comes in. (I recently heard of a student who was actually looking for "Mr. Bursar.") This is the office that takes the money for your tuition and other expenses. *Always* pay attention to any messages—email or letters—from the bursar: they mean money! Some time may be allowed between signing up for your classes and paying your bill, but once the payment deadlines have passed, you may no longer be allowed to be enrolled in the courses you signed up for.

Explore payment plans that can make the process less painful and more organized according to your own needs and budget. The bursar is often willing to work with you and the financial aid office, within reason. You have to ask.

The calendar for payment is typically posted on the Web, sent in a message to your (campus) email address, or even sent to you in the mail, sometimes more than once. You or your parents are responsible for paying the bills.

Measles Immunization

All students, but especially those returning to school as adults or who are not native born, must meet the state or local requirement for **pre-matriculation immunization** for measles. Measles is a highly contagious disease, and campuses are easy places for it to spread. Many states require proof of immunization, and usually require evidence that you have had immunization shots within a prescribed time period or that you have had the disease. Once immunized, either by injection or having had the disease, you should be fine for the future, but be sure to hold on to the evidence. If you have no such evidence from a medical doctor, then you must get the shots, which may be administered on campus or by your own medical practitioner within a designated time frame. Not meeting this requirement may mean that the college drops your registration, as the school itself may otherwise be subject to fees or fines for not complying with the law. Again, pay attention to messages from the college, and be sure that you have met all the requirements for admission.

IF YOU HAVE A PROBLEM

Be sure to get to know your school's rules and processes. Pay attention at orientations or during the first-year seminar. You won't be let off the hook easily if you miss deadlines or fall afoul of the rules. The farther along you are in your college career, the less tolerance the school will have for you getting it wrong.

While you can sometimes **appeal** a misstep to whatever body your school designates (deans and/or advisors), integrity and evidence of real misunderstanding or a situation beyond your control must be present for you to have even a glimmer of hope that your appeal may have a positive outcome. They will look for evidence that you are not a repeat offender or gaming the system.

If you seek an appeal, it is a good idea to first talk to an advisor to see what your chances are and how you might best present your case if it is legitimate. There may be forbearance when the situation is beyond your control or a clear error (you registered for the wrong class because you hit the wrong computer key, or were unable to get faculty approval to get into a class because the professor was away, for example). Usually the rules for any appeals process are published on the Web, on forms, or in the advising center or registrar's office.

Remember that, among many things, college is teaching you to be self-sufficient, so the onus will be on you to learn, know, and follow the rules of your campus processes. When you graduate, no one will be there to tell you to pay your bills or explain how to do insurance planning. You learn these skills now by navigating through college. Good luck!

Chapter 4
WHICH COURSES?

THE CAREER AND MAJORS CONNECTION

Many, if not most, persons think of college as a direct alignment with a future career path. It is not. You do not have to major in biology to be a medical doctor, in political science to be a lawyer, or in economics for a career in business.

But will college lead to success in a career? Yes! You will earn 74 percent more with a college degree than without one. These are not contradictory ideas, though, and understanding them will help you figure out how to choose your courses.

First, you need to rethink the idea of a career. What *is* a career? The dictionary defines it as a long-term occupational activity, where a job is defined as a paid activity. Raking leaves is a job; landscaping is a career. A *career path* implies ever-increasing levels of knowledge and skill in a particular arena.

Many decades ago a career path was assumed to mean that you would join a firm and move up a hierarchical ladder during forty years or so, holding a variety of *jobs,* and then retire from that firm, having reached whatever peak your capacities and interests allowed. You could have moved up in the same area of expertise, which would constitute a career in that area of specialization. For example, a junior accountant could become the head of the accounting department—that would constitute a career in accounting.

Or you could have moved around to different departments in the same firm, having a career in that industry, but holding many kinds of jobs in it.

A Story: Myra

Myra started college having loved the sciences in high school. Her ambition was to work at NASA one day. By the end of her first college year, however, she was less engaged by her science courses and more with sociology and urban affairs. Since those were areas near and dear to her father, they seemed interesting. She liked the feel of changing the world. Then she discovered philosophy. She fell in love with the abstractions, logic, and play of ideas and the theories of how human beings think and reason. As a junior, she majored in the field and wrote a brilliant senior thesis, which brought her respect in her department; she even served as a student representative on a faculty search committee.

While her parents wondered how she would use her degree, Myra finds that all of her interests remain important to her. She reads science for fun and applies it to her volunteer work in food safety and the environment. She works as a fund-raiser for urban causes, thus working for social change every day. And she uses skills she learned as a philosophy major in her research and writing, as well as in understanding the world around her.

But if you think about the work histories of individuals you know, very few have followed this path. And the younger your circle of acquaintances is, the less likely its members are to have stayed with one employer or even in the same field.

Since the 1980s, the idea of secure, long-term employment has disappeared. Employees at every level of the hierarchy became vulnerable to layoffs. Even CEOs began to turn over at a greater rate. In the case of younger persons entering the workplace—having seen their parents laid off—the ethos of employee expendability came to be dominant, replacing the idea of owing an employer lifetime loyalty. And as companies stretched globally and shut down domestically, we all began to think in terms of moving wherever our skills and talents could be most valued and used in a variety of contexts.

Additionally, it is difficult to predict what new industries or opportunities may emerge. In the past few years, the Internet, the environment, and biotechnology have all generated new careers and opportunities that did not exist before. Most students think of a small handful of job titles, such as doctor, lawyer, businessperson, teacher, or engineer. But if you look at **monster.com** or the Labor Department's *Occupational Outlook Handbook* (**www.bls.gov/OCO/**)—both great resources—you will find a huge array of job titles that you never knew existed; new ones are created daily to meet changing social and economic needs. Over a lifetime you may hold many job titles.

Right now the fields that are creating the most demand are in technology and science, followed by the environment and energy, health care–related fields—including management and medical areas—and education. Among other fields, marketing, publishing, news, and media—including the hardware and software used in these businesses—are undergoing huge transformations, which ultimately always creates new opportunities once the dust settles. As noted above, such sweeping changes make it almost impossible to predict today what jobs will develop.

So what does college prepare you for? College can give you the basic skills that will allow you to adapt to a changing world and even to retool job-specific skills as the need arises.

Let me give two examples. My own career is one. I majored in political science in college, where one of the skills I learned was writing (lots of long papers). My first job was teaching junior high school, my second was in advertising management, and my next in corporate public affairs, where I moved up the ladder and then moved to marketing in the same firm. I left that company and became a consultant on work-family issues and then on entrepreneurship. I next ended up working at a college. I earned a doctorate and moved up the ladder on an academic career path, which has led me to write this book. The skills I used from college relate to writing and communications, research, and understanding politics and power in any organizational context.

In graduate school you most likely will specialize in the area where most of your work life will be located. But think in terms of less than a lifetime. Remember to be open to change, even returning to school to take a course or earn a certificate as new opportunities emerge or your own interests change, as mine did. As with all aspects of your life, aim for your work life to be dynamic and full of growth, not static. College is not an end—it is a beginning.

Interestingly, as undergraduates more leaders have liberal arts degrees than specialized degrees, including undergraduate business degrees. The liberal arts are a strong preparation for the varied careers you may have along life's path.

Info: Liberal Arts

The term actually refers to colleges offering a degree in a course of study comprising the arts and humanities, natural sciences, and social sciences (which may not have direct vocational relevance). The **social sciences** generally relate to the study of human experience, society, and social behavior. They include psychology, sociology, anthropology, history, political science, and economics. The **humanities** are generally the subjects that relate to humans as intellectual and creative beings. These typically include literature, languages (English as well as all others), philosophy, and the arts, such as fine arts, music, and dance, as well as the histories of these subjects. The **sciences** comprise a course of study of the physical or material world, explored through a rigorous and systematic process. They include biology, physics, chemistry, mathematics, engineering, and computer science. Some courses or majors cross over several of these categories and are called interdisciplinary; they might include social psychology, for example, which crosses sociological issues with those of psychology.

The advantage of a liberal arts education is that you develop a range of skills that will serve you well for the rest of your life. Some courses focus on reading and writing, others expose you to different methods of doing research to prove points, and each subject area requires different analytical and critical thinking skills. All together they help shape a person capable of growing into leadership and creatively meeting challenges.

So, if you love learning, a liberal arts degree will give you the richest range of experiences. Dean Matthew Santirocco at New York University's College of Arts and Sciences, in speaking of the liberal arts, once put it this way: "Its goal is less to convey a body of knowledge than to present the chief approaches to understanding our world...[I]t should develop in you the breadth, agility, and flexibility that will enable you to embark on a lifetime of learning and to adapt to a rapidly changing world. In fact, seen in this way, the liberal arts are an eminently *practical* education."

My favorite example of this view is the story of the late civil rights and feminist activist Pauli Murray. Murray was born in the South in the early 1900s, and as a Black woman with a college degree at that time, her only career choice was to teach. She became quite aware, after many years, that her students were greatly affected by what happened in their family lives. She left teaching and earned a master's degree in social work with the aim of improving families' lives. In the process she came to feel that the social and legal systems stood in the way of her peoples' ability to progress, and so she left social work and earned a law degree. She became well known as a civil rights and women's rights attorney. When she was in her sixties she began to believe that the key to a good life lay in the spiritual realm. She returned to school and earned a divinity degree, and at age seventy-two became a minister and the "Priest-in-Charge" of the Holy Nativity Church in Baltimore.

Pauli Murray had four distinct and productive careers over a long life span that continued into her eighties.

THE MAJOR

As in Pauli Murray's case, you too can have many different careers and many more jobs during your life span. Your choice of major in college will not limit your options—unless you pick one that is not suited to you, then it will.

A **major** is a subject area in which you choose to concentrate. It is characterized as a **discipline**, which is a specific body of knowledge and inquiry. Each major has a different approach to its subject, but they all are valid modes of learning both information and skills.

As stated earlier, your major doesn't dictate your career. Many of you may believe that you must major in biology as preparation for becoming a medical doctor—not true. You do have to study biology, chemistry, organic chemistry, physics, and math to qualify for medical school. But today, most medical school students have majored in history or philosophy. Similarly, law schools, as pointed out, don't particularly seek students who have majored in political science or law-oriented courses as undergraduates. Corporate leaders come from majors as diverse as English and history and psychology, where they learn communications skills and what makes people tick. The students in professional or graduate schools have two things in common: They had strong GPAs and strong scores on the tests required for admission to graduate programs. Some of the tests required for graduate programs are the Medical College Admissions Test (MCAT) for medicine, Graduate Record Exam (GRE) for graduate school, Law School Admissions Test (LSAT) for law, and Graduate Management Admissions Test (GMAT) for business school.

To achieve these results, which will at least start you toward a career path, you need to choose an academic path that allows you to excel. That means doing what you already love. If you love poetry, then major in English. If you love math, then major in that. If you are passionate about several subjects, major in one and minor in another. A **minor** allows you to undertake a concentration in a disciplinary area without the intense focus and requirements of a major. (A major takes the *major*ity of your time and a minor less, or the *minor*ity of it.) Or you may choose an **interdisciplinary major** such as American Studies, which embraces multiple disciplines, or neuropsychology, which includes both biology and psychology.

Students sometimes say that it felt like cheating to take what came easily to them, but doing what comes easily gives you a chance to show your full capacities—you at your best. Your advising or career office may have resources, such as tests, that can show you where your strengths and interests align. Check with these offices.

Some students are frustrated that they are having difficulty making up their minds on a major. They do well in several areas and have a broad range of interests. The truth is more than half of any freshman class is undecided. This is often a sign of intellectual breadth, a good thing. I have known bio majors who wrote fiction, religion majors who loved science, dance majors with economic minors. (Some of these students selected one of the interdisciplinary majors, which allowed for more flexibility.) I have even known faculty who, during the course of their careers, taught sculpture and economics, taught English literature and wrote food reviews, taught math and philosophy.

There is nothing wrong with being multifaceted and talented in more than one area. One of the purposes of college is to show students, many of whom think they know what they want to do, all the other things there are to learn. Expect to change your mind about your probable major during your first two years. Again, remember that your major coupled with a broad general education will assure you the skills necessary for your work life, but also knowledge that contributes to your personal development and life-long pursuit of learning.

Your **college advising office** will help you devise a plan to get you through the required classes of the core curriculum and guide you to a plan for your major, minor, and electives that will help you maximize your time and assets. Many students do not take full advantage of the advisors available and get trapped in inappropriate classes or academic pathways that do not serve them well in the long term. Particularly if you are a transfer student or an older or nontraditional student, you must use this guidance so that your time and money are well spent.

Skill Building

But what about preparing for a career? What you need are skills. You also need evidence that you are intelligent and learn quickly and easily. Your grades provide this evidence.

We live in a fast-changing environment. You need to show good grades in a variety of subjects and excellence in the majority of your courses. You need to show that you can find, absorb, and integrate lots of information. (Most employers want to train or teach you to do things their way, anyway.) Sometimes you may need to engage in "thinking outside of the box." If you're studying a subject you love, then you are able to do these things more easily than if you're struggling to understand the basic concepts of a subject area.

Employers also tell us that they seek, in addition to basic quantitative skills, really solid communications skills. You must be able to write—presentations, memos, reports, speeches that must be clear, logical, cogent, literate (good grammar and spelling), and persuasive. Courses that require heavy reading and writing many pages of papers are good practice for an executive career path. President Obama won the 2008 election in part on his verbal skills. Students who score well on the MCAT, GMAT, LSAT, and GRE do so as much on the basis of the tests' verbal sections as they do on other content. A major in history or English comes in here. I have known English literature majors with 3.9 GPAs who got job offers at prestigious financial services firms. These companies recognized strong communications skills and grade point averages as evidence of intelligence, diligence, and teachableness.

Firms also want individuals who can be good team players and quickly learn how things are done, i.e., those with good people skills who are, again, teachable. If you major in people-centered subjects like sociology, psychology, or anthropology, to name a few, then you will learn more about human behavior. But history and literature, economics and political science are also studies in human behavior. All these subject areas can help build skills useful in understanding situations and colleagues in the workplace.

Of course, what builds people skills is interaction with others (obvious, yes?). But if you select a major that does not suit your style of learning, interests, or capacities, you will spend hours in study and have little time to engage in social or extracurricular activities that allow you to build the leadership and human interaction skills that are an essential part of a successful work life.

Employers also seek individuals possessing critical thinking skills who can anticipate solutions to potential problems. Any major will enable you to develop those skills. All learning involves discovering new knowledge and solutions to hard questions. How things work and why and how they have worked in the past make up the essence of academic inquiry. Engaging in research, whether in a library or a lab, is how critical thinking skills are developed. The questions faculty ask to get you to think are designed to build this capacity. Again, if you are studying what you love, you will be asking and answering tough questions because they interest you.

You must also have some degree of quantitative aptitude. Students come with varying degrees of natural skill in this area. Perhaps you would rather deal with numbers, spatial relations, or abstract quantitative concepts than read a novel or historical text. Or perhaps you instead develop quantitative skills in school with varying degrees of success. Either way, whether you're managing a budget, developing a media plan based on metrics, or designing a house, you need math in some form. If it is your passion, then it can be a major or minor or a significant ingredient in your chosen subject, such as physics. I know an English professor who has traced the role of math in literature. Musical aptitude and mathematical ability are often coupled. However you approach it, you can be sure it is useful knowledge.

A Cautionary Tale: Paul and the Right Major

Paul's family had decided that he should be a doctor, believed in their Caribbean homeland to be the highest calling one could have. Paul was a great student and athlete and so had his pick of colleges. Once enrolled in a fine school, he followed his family's wishes and declared himself premed. But every term he struggled with the array of required math and science courses. He almost lost his place on the soccer team as his grades slid to a dangerously low level. By his junior year, he knew in his heart that he did not want to be a doctor—compared to bio and chem, and especially the physics he was now taking, he had done well in and really enjoyed his history classes, taken to fulfill core requirements and as electives along the way. In fact he was close to failing physics. If he did, he would definitely be off the team. In the back of his mind he had the idea of a career in sports management.

Paul finally went to the dean and shared his fear of tanking in physics. In the course of the conversation, he revealed that he did not really want to be a doctor or to major in chemistry. The dean checked his record and noted the number of history classes; she called the department chair and was able to switch his major. She also persuaded his parents that either a law or business degree could lead to a prestigious career (perhaps in sports management).

Paul took an internship in the sports field and wrote a thesis relating to sports history. His grades went way up, and he was accepted to law school, where he found that he had a new passion and talent: Instead of an MD, Paul became a DA and is now a U.S. Attorney.

Lessons learned: Major in what you care about. Get support from deans or advisors in working with your family to make choices or changes. Don't wait until a crisis occurs to get the help and support you need.

Info: Leadership Intangibles

Q: Let's talk about hiring. What are you looking for in a job candidate?

A: Typically when you are hiring a vice-president of a company they already have the résumé and they have the experience base. And so what you are trying to find out are the intangibles of leadership, communication style, and the ability to, today, adapt to change.

And there are a lot of ways to go at that. I like to ask people what they've read, what are the last three or four books they've read, and what did they enjoy about those.

—From an interview with Richard Anderson, CEO, Delta Airlines, New York Times, *April 26, 2009.*

THE CURRICULUM

Most persons do not enter college aware of all the course offerings or even inclined to take subjects that might make them feel insecure or ignorant. So colleges design curricula ("courses of study," expressed in Latin) that allow for exploration of many subject areas—and that provide basic skills in areas to help students become employable.

The first two years of college are usually spent in **required courses** that students always grumble about. These classes may be clustered in what is called a **core curriculum**. The faculty has deliberated about the basic knowledge all students should have, regardless of their proclivity toward a particular subject area. Faculty also want to be sure that all students are exposed to subjects entirely new to them that could be wonderful unexpected arenas for learning. Many students taking their first course in anthropology, philosophy, physics, or sociology find the subject fascinating and want to go back for more, or even pursue the field as a livelihood. But if a core curriculum requiring some exposure to a variety of subjects had not existed, their delights would have gone undiscovered. By requiring such courses, the risk factor is removed—the school has done you a favor.

The other reality is that college is the last chance you will have for a long time to engage in purely intellectual play. Once you move on to work or graduate study, your focus is on the subjects that enhance your work needs. But for now a broad spectrum of courses is laid before you to enjoy, in part for their own sake and in part for the skills and background they can contribute toward your career success. Rather than being the waste of time many students think it is, the core curriculum not only moves you toward skill building, but offers exposure to new fields where, much to your own surprise, you may excel. If you examine each of the disciplines in the course offerings and required curriculum, you will find that each is also useful for whatever path your life may take.

A Story: David

David began as the typical premed-oriented biology major, but he struggled fiercely with the subjects involved, nearly destroying his GPA. The mandated core curriculum, however, introduced him to a foreign language, Italian, and to philosophy; he changed majors and salvaged his GPA. Many years later he ended up taking the science classes again as a **postbacc** (usually a special program offering targeted undergraduate courses to someone who has earned a baccalaureate degree [BA or BS] already) and did well. He is now a medical doctor who loves visiting Italy. His experience was enriched and his career potential fulfilled because of required courses he took as an undergraduate.

Writing and Communications

You have to learn to read better and faster, and to write well, in order to succeed in college and in life. None of us is ever perfect, though, and even the best writers look to editors to help them refine their texts.

As a freshman in college, you'll take a course in literature or writing that is aimed at enhancing whatever skill level you have brought to college. Usually the writing you have done in high school is limited and may not require research and critical thought. This is the difference between what you wrote then and what you might write in professional life or graduate training. Many more pages are expected. You will have to learn how to find source material and how to cite it. You will have to engage in self-expression, which is different from repeating what the instructor has told you. You will have to articulate a premise and defend it, using evidence. And there may be chances for creative expression.

If you're lucky, you'll be required to do more than the freshman writing course and will have to take additional courses that enable you to develop those skills more fully. You should not be able to graduate without knowing how to write well. (Many do, but their career paths are affected.) Effective communication is both written and verbal, and a worthwhile course also offers the chance to make presentations before others. Texting, email, and Twitter are informal subsets of communications skills. They reflect back on you—your intelligence and your level of maturity. Appearing sloppy or illiterate, even in emails, can hurt your career. Take your writing classes seriously.

Mathematics

As noted, you will require some quantitative skills in life, whether when budgeting for home or business or helping your offspring with math homework. While your calculator may do the computations, you need to understand the underlying concepts.

The work life you encounter or embrace will usually require higher-level skills. If you own a business, you must calculate your profit-and-loss statements. As a marketer you may have to figure out market share ratios. Certainly professionals in accounting or finance, and also in science, need strong quantitative skills. Reasoning skills and accuracy are also key.

Colleges usually require you to take math at some level. You may take a placement test, which determines your strengths and your best fit for courses. Your high school transcript, read by someone knowledgeable, helps determine where you belong in the early math class offerings. Often math is a prerequisite for other courses such as chemistry, economics, or accounting. If you do not have the basic math skills, you cannot succeed in more advanced courses in these areas, which rely on concepts you should have mastered earlier.

Math is often considered a gateway subject because early failure in it can limit other options. If (as with me) it is not your strength, or your high school did not offer higher-level work in it, then you need to seek out the help available through tutors or faculty support.

Foreign Languages

It is almost trite now to say that we are a global economy. International relations pervade every aspect of our lives. And the path to the chief executive's seat these days usually involves a stop in some foreign posting.

Yet often in the United States, unless you are a student for whom English is a second language, little or no effort to learn other languages is evident. People in other countries learn several languages as a matter of course. I have acquaintances who think nothing of knowing as many as five. Spanish, Chinese, French, Russian, and Arabic are all languages that can be professionally useful. Many students find that studying Latin is a good way to learn grammar and a gateway to other Romance languages (French, Italian, Spanish), which have Latin as a root. And at the least, it is fun to know Italian when traveling in Italy or ordering in an Italian restaurant. A good college requires you to show proficiency in two languages (English and another). Take advantage of this opportunity—perhaps even apply the skill in a semester abroad.

The Humanities

The humanities are courses that include the arts (visual—painting, sculpture—music, dance, theater) as well as literature, philosophy, and cultural studies, which reveal how human beings interpret our world. You learn to understand how to view a painting or make one, how to hear music or create it, how value systems have emerged and influence our behavior—in short, what makes us human. The humanities fields contain hard facts but are also rich in interpretation.

You may think these are impractical courses and wonder why they are mandated in a well-rounded curriculum. The answer is: the ability to engage in analytical thinking supported by solid reasoning and evidence comprises the skill set one gains from the humanities. This is the skill set of leaders. And you may also just enjoy the music along the way.

Social Sciences

This group of courses teaches how human beings behave from a more scientific standpoint—gathering evidence, observing patterns, reading behaviors. The subjects include sociology, psychology, political science, anthropology, archeology, economics, and history (sometimes considered a humanities field).

In the social sciences, one learns how to collect and read data, an eminently useful skill. Though valued for their own sake, these subjects are highly practical foundations for marketing, management, law, and finance. Firms use anthropologists to understand the cultures of foreign markets; psychology can be useful in advertising or human resources management; and a sociological perspective on behavior can aid in building effective workplaces. On the other hand, some students favor these fields to make sense of their own worlds, using psychology as a gateway to the self or political science to understand power relations.

Sciences

The physical sciences (biology, chemistry, physics, engineering, and their subsets) are also driven by gathering observable evidence. Experimentation to gather proof of how the universe functions in all its physical aspects can be exciting.

It is difficult today to engage in the discourses of civil society without having some scientific literacy. You cannot understand the debates about stem cells, the impact of green technologies, or even strategies affecting your own health unless you have been exposed to the sciences in a meaningful way.

Other Perspectives on the Curriculum

You will find that all of these subjects and disciplines are intertwined. A large urban university once offered an experimental course taught by faculty from English, biology, and urban studies, to look at rivers. The poets and novelists saw rivers as metaphors for life, the biologists were interested in the physical life in the rivers, and the urbanists looked at the ways the rivers shaped our urban lives. All are valid viewpoints, and any subject can be approached from many disciplinary lenses. No subject is a waste of time.

One of the ways you can see how coursework is relevant is to take one or two that include a **service learning** component, where your work applies to a project serving a local community. For example, many campuses have Engineers Without Borders programs—students do actual projects that, for instance, provide swings for disabled children or water in a community on the African continent.

A core curriculum lets you explore many disciplines while you decide which one appeals most to your learning style and which subjects intrigue you. At the same time, your view of the world and your skills are broadening. What you learn and are exposed to will be of benefit to you in your work and your life, even if it is not totally clear now as to how. Talk to alumni who have been out of school for some period of time and you will see.

Hard or Easy?

Any endeavor can be turned into a difficult experience. If you choose a major or concentrate on courses that do not fit your learning style, or for which you do not have strong preparation, then these courses will be hard for you. But they may be easy for someone else.

Courses that come easy to you are a function of their fit for you. If you are a quantitative thinker (good with numbers) and hate writing, then you may want to focus on courses that require more quantitative work and less writing. On the other hand, if writing is your asset, then the opposite will be true. However, as noted earlier, you will need both skill sets in your life and career, so if one is not your strength, be sure to get extra help in it rather than avoiding it altogether (not that you would be allowed to do so!). Whether you choose a "hard or easy" major is a personal matter, for the most part, but there are always circumstances that can affect your choices.

Some professors are "hard." That is to say, they require lots of reading or assignments or pitch their lectures at a high level of understanding, and they have high standards and expectations. My mother-in-law was considered a hard teacher. Her syllabus went on for pages and required her students to read a huge number of books. She didn't allow grammatical errors, and you had to do the homework. Her students were terrified of her. She could be fierce, but years later these same students said they had learned more from her than from any other teacher and would always remember it. My own students often complained that I made them read too much, but they later understood why all the work made sense. Some of the best teachers are demanding and expect the most and the best of you. Do not shun them because they have this sort of reputation. A course can be challenging but worthwhile.

You can find out what other students have thought of professors by reading course evaluations, which are often posted on college websites. (I caution about using those such as **http://blog.ratemyprofessors.com**—postings are often by the grumpy students who may not have gotten the easy A they were seeking.) You can also, probably more appropriately and reliably, ask seniors who are majoring in your area of interest, to see what their experiences have been. They can tell you if the professor in question is fair, accessible, passionate, and knowledgeable and thus worth a bit more rigor for the value of the experience.

If you're looking for easy courses in order to get a higher GPA, note that graduate schools tend to see through that ploy. Medical schools, for example, do not like it when a student enrolled in a rigorous college takes organic chemistry (notoriously challenging) during the summer at a less rigorous school. Whether you are going on to graduate school or a career, being able to point to courses that take a bit more effort but in which you did well speaks volumes about you and your perseverance in the face of a tough situation. Isn't that the person *you* would want to hire, rather than someone looking for an easy way out?

However, you can make your life hard by taking too many courses in a rush to graduate or because many of the classes you want to take are all offered in one term. A normal courseload, depending on how the credits are allocated at your school, is three or four classes. Fewer than that and you may, in fact, be considered part-time, which can impact your financial aid eligibility. Taking more than that can push the limits of what you can do well.

I have known a few extraordinarily gifted and well-organized students who have managed as many as three majors and a near perfect GPA. But they did not have much of a life and/or lived on no sleep. This approach is not advisable. If you work part-time, have family responsibilities, or are involved in more than one extracurricular activity—a club, fraternity, or community service work—then you must pace yourself or your work suffers. Again, a sought-after employer wants to see a 3.6 GPA, plus internships, leadership roles, and service. That can only be accomplished if you are taking the right number of courses in the area that is right for you.

You don't want to race through college, but you also don't want to string it out too long. It's important to note that if you take too long to complete your degree, you may lose your eligibility for financial aid, which requires that you show reasonable progress toward completion of the degree. Dropping too many courses or signing up for too few, in hopes of protecting your GPA, can drop you to part-time status, where you are not eligible for aid. Pacing yourself, then, is really important in many ways. Your academic advising office will be a big help to you with these matters.

Info: Grades

Grades are important, but you need to understand them for what they measure and what they mean. Grades are measures of performance, reflecting how well you have understood material, done assignments according to instructions, and engaged in the class. Often but not always, professors will spell out in the syllabus how they calculate a grade—particular percentages, for instance, for quizzes, papers, class participation, and final exams. If the elements are not spelled out, you can ask for a breakdown. Having such information will make it possible for you to keep track of how you are doing in a class, and you will be able to calculate the kind of grades you may get based on what you have done relative to each of the elements being graded.

There are three different aspects of your overall **grade point average (GPA)**:

- the final grade for a course (calculated based on all the elements making up grades received)
- the number of credits for a course
- the number of courses taken

Professors evaluate your papers and exams or quizzes as alphabetic or numeric grades, so you could get an A or a 92 on a paper, for example. The final grade will generally be submitted as a letter. That is then translated into another set of numbers, with A equal to 4, B to 3, C to 2, D to 1, and F to 0. Your GPA, both for the semester and for the whole time you are in school, is an average of these numbers based on the number of credits you have taken. The GPA is also adjusted and weighted according to the number of credits a course represents.

To get the GPA for a semester or year, the point value of each grade is multiplied by the credit hours the course is worth. This yields the grade point value of the course. So a four-credit course will weigh more than a two-credit course. These grade points are then added up and divided by the total number of credit hours to determine your grade point average. Your registrar will figure this for you, and your average will show on your transcript at the end of each term. Online grade calculators, however, will allow you to project what you need to do to achieve a higher GPA. Doing this for yourself periodically is useful as a reality check. You can see how many A's you will need, for example, to bring a 2.5 GPA to a 3.3 range.

Colleges have varying grading systems, which are usually letter grades—A, B, C, D, F—and perhaps subsets of these—A+, A, A–, B+, B, B–, C+, C, C–, D, and F. The latter is called a suffix grading system because of the plus or minus suffixes. Note that D rarely has plus or minus signs and F never does. The A+ is also uncommon. The advantage of this system is that it allows more precision in grading. If you relate the letter grades to numerical scores on a scale of 100 to 60 (below 60 is generally a failing grade, or F) then an A would be in the 90 to 100 range, a B in the 80 to 90, a C in the 70 to 80, a D in the 60 to 70, and all numbers below that failing. In this system's more precise ranges, for example, a B+ would be 87 to 90 and a B– 83 and below. Not having suffixes may be to the advantage of the student at the lower end of the grading scale, because a 70 is equal to a 79. But the suffix system works to the advantage of the stronger student, as a B+ looks better than a B and in the final numerical analysis counts for more as well.

Grades reflect how hard you work, how well you know the material, and perhaps also whether you have chosen the right field or course of study for yourself. Grades are not given out lightly, and in fact, grading is one of the more difficult things faculty have to contend with. They must plan their courses knowing how the grade structure will be built. They must seek ways to assure objectivity, so that they can defend their grading decisions if necessary, especially in more interpretive courses, like in the humanities. Grading papers or other work that can be objectively measured, such as right or wrong answers in math, is more straightforward.

It does not serve you well to demand certain grades because you want or need them. If you have not done the work, done well on tasks assigned, or engaged in class activities, you cannot expect a professor to change a C grade to a B because, say, your scholarship is at risk.

If you are working like crazy on your own, but not doing well, it may be a signal that you need to get more help from professors or tutors or even study groups. If you are struggling to get good grades in a category of courses that you may think could be your major, then that field may be a bad choice for you. As has been said elsewhere in this book, the courses that seem easy may be the ones where you are playing to your strengths, interests, and aptitudes—where higher grades come with less effort because you "get it." And concentrating on those courses should be where you will be best served. This is where you will be able to build a strong GPA.

An easy way to tell how ready you are for a particular course is to find out the way course levels are organized at your school. If you are a first-year student, most of your courses are labeled at the 100 level or designated as introductory classes. A 400-level course is meant for seniors or those deeply into their majors. Classes at the 200 and 300 levels typically are for second- and third-year students, and not meant for beginners. Each level represents an increasing body of knowledge and competency—skills build on one another. So in a 100-level biology class you are learning the basic skills you'll need to do the work of all the other classes that follow. If you try to skip ahead, you'll be lost without the previous knowledge. It seems obviously unworkable, but I have seen students try to make a schedule work by enrolling in whatever is offered in a time slot, regardless of appropriateness.

Many courses state that **prerequisites** are required, so you cannot make the mistake of leaping ahead—you may have to take certain courses first or pass a placement test to show you know key information or processes. Pay attention to these sequences. If you are a transfer student, be sure to determine if you have already taken courses that are the equivalent of pre-requisites or other requirements. The admissions or advising office offers **transfer credit** advice, though decisions about equivalency are made by the relevant department, which has the expertise in the field. In some cases there are agreements (known as **articulation agreements**) between schools that make these processes easier, especially within a state or local college system. Ask about them, as they can save you time. If you're transferring, remember to hold on to all your documentation. You may need to show transcripts, course descriptions, or syllabi in the process of getting transfer credits.

Bailing Out

If you find yourself in over your head, there are ways to deal with the situation. First, always pay attention to the college calendar deadline for **dropping a class**. Dropping a class should be the last option you take. Usually the last day to drop is several weeks before the end of a term. Schools do not allow students to take a course, stack up quiz and paper scores, and then decide at the last minute to drop.

If the deadline has already passed, at that point you'll have to do exceedingly well on whatever assignments are still coming due or else deal with a grade that may not be desirable. Alternatively, you may be able to negotiate an **incomplete** with the instructor if you have good reason for your problems, such as illness. In such a case, a final paper or project would be deferred for a specific time period. This is done only at the professor's discretion, and if you still then fail to get the work done by the date agreed upon you can fail the class.

It's important to be aware that at the beginning of a term there is usually a time (maybe two weeks) when you can **drop and add** courses without penalty. During this time, you can see if there is good chemistry between you and your professors or whether a class interests you or is the right level.

Another strategy to employ is taking courses **pass/fail**. Many schools allow you to exercise this option in a limited number of courses over your college career. You do all the work but do not risk a low grade. This can be useful if you want to take a class that seems interesting but perhaps challenging, and you do not want to jeopardize your GPA. You may also do this if you know you can pass, but will not do it with a grade much beyond a C. If pass/fail is an option on your campus, there are usually specific procedures to follow and time frames for declaring this. Check your catalog.

Pass/fail is not meant for key courses—the physics or organic chemistry class you must take as a premed, for example. Medical schools consider it a weasel strategy and frown on it. Indeed too many pass/fails on a transcript can signal fear or laziness to a grad school or employer. But if you're a physics major with a great average and you want to take that fascinating Russian lit class from a famous professor, you might want to do it pass/fail. It is a choice to enhance your enjoyment and not to boost (or harm) your GPA.

As the term progresses, you may realize that you have made a mistake, or the mix of classes is overwhelming and you need to let one go, or your job hours change. When you decide that you do need to drop a class, you must formally **withdraw**. This means seeing your advisor or the registrar. In fact, *before* you make the decision, discuss it with any or all of them to see what your options are. Again we remind you, following the deadlines in the school's academic calendar is crucial in making such decisions.

Do *not* stop attending without formally letting the professors, your advisor, or a dean know. Disappearing from a course can cause you many problems. If you withdraw by disappearing, an F may appear on your record. You are also likely held accountable for the course tuition bill, even if the professor has not seen you all term. An F affects your GPA and perhaps your financial aid, and the bill disrupts the careful budgeting you've done to continue your education.

If you disappear, professors, especially in large classes, will just believe you did not do the work. They do not know if you are gone for good for a legitimate reason or if you plan to show up for the final to get a grade (some students do try this, and faculty frown on it). Obviously, where class participation influences a grade, not appearing will count against you.

If you formally withdraw from a class, usually a W appears on your transcript. It is a neutral designation and only becomes significant if you develop a pattern of Ws or if you cannot offer a reasonable explanation. Think like the person looking at a transcript: Do several Ws signal someone who runs from tough situations?

Withdrawing isn't usually the best course. It is best to hang in there. Talk to your professor about what is hard for you. Seek out tutoring if it is available (it will be) or create study groups with those who seem on more solid ground. More on such strategies appears later, in chapter 8 (Time Management and Study Skills).

The one exception, when you may be able to withdraw without penalty from one or more classes well into a semester, is a verifiable personal crisis—a death in the family, your own illness. Do not lie about this though. In such situations, schools have the right to ask for doctor's notes or death certificates. Talk honestly to school officials as soon as possible so that you can take the appropriate actions and get the support you need if you have to withdraw from any courses. This approach will make your school life much easier.

A Cautionary Tale:
Cheryl's Withdrawal without Notice

In the early fall, Cheryl was called home from school because her mother was seriously ill. She returned to school, but her heart stayed home, and eventually she was actually needed back at home. She left her classes without notice and took care of her brothers and sisters and cared for her mother until her health improved.

During the summer, Cheryl began to receive notices that she owed money to the college. She had had a scholarship, but was required to maintain a good GPA to hold it. By dropping out without notice she had gotten Fs in all her courses, and her GPA had fallen through the floor. She lost the scholarship, had a terrible record, and now owed the school money.

If she had told her advisor about her mother's problems, Cheryl could have submitted a formal withdrawal and taken a leave of absence, which would have protected her grades and also her scholarship. She ended up having to provide evidence of her mother's illness and the time frame involved in her care, as part of a process of having the courses (and the F grades) removed from her transcript and reinstating her scholarship. In the fall she was able to resume her studies, but she had learned a lesson along the way.

Lessons learned: Do not drop out without telling your advisor and your professors, as well as filing the proper forms. Let someone know when you are having a crisis.

ACADEMIC ENRICHMENT PROGRAMS AND HONORS

You need to always keep in mind that college prepares you for a life well lived and enriched by many forms of new knowledge. But you are also looking for the employment goal at the end of the process. This is the reason you want to keep your record clear of too many Ws, avoid any evidence of bad behavior, and, most important, do well academically.

Schools offer many additional opportunities to excel academically. They are not necessarily tied to the classroom, but they also build and enhance your professional profile. Programs range from special internships (sometimes coupled with a class) to mentored research fellowships to summer experiences that may take you abroad or away from home. Some are affiliated with your campus, others such as **SPUR** (Summer Programs for Undergraduate Research) may be located at other schools that could be potential sites for your graduate study.

There are many federally funded programs for students classified as low income, first generation, or underrepresented in certain fields, and the students they typically seek include, specifically, Blacks, Latinos, Native Americans, the disabled, or in some cases women in general or veterans.

One such is the McNair program, funded by the Department of Education and named for Ronald McNair, a Black astronaut lost on the 1986 *Challenger* flight. It is one of the Federal Trio Programs, originally three and now eight programs designed to support students from disadvantaged backgrounds. The McNair and programs like it—including NIMH/COR (National Institute of Mental Health–Career Opportunities in Research Program), MARC (National Institute of Health's Minority Access to Research Careers Program), MBRS (National Institute of Health's Minority Biomedical Research Program), RISE (National Institute of Health's Research Initiative for Scientific Enhancement Program), LSAMP (Louis Stokes Alliance for Minority Participation Programs in Science, Technology, Engineering and Math), and many others—hope to give students in the designated populations access to mentored research opportunities on their campuses, summer GRE prep, special courses or workshops, and exposure to conferences and opportunities to give presentations, as well as general guidance to graduate programs. Even better, they usually offer stipends, sometimes sizeable ones. They commonly recruit students as rising juniors who have GPAs at or above 3.0 and who show passion and promise for academic work above the undergraduate level.

These programs are gateways to other opportunities. They help build your credentials for future employers and professional or graduate programs because they are competitive and show what others think of you. Winning a slot is an enormous honor; being nominated or considered is also an honor. These programs provide support, skills, and networks, and program directors are a source of nurturance and individualized guidance. Not every campus has a full menu of offerings, so see the advising or financial aid offices or your major department for information. Application processes and deadlines vary as well from campus to campus.

When applying for special programs, you are required to write a **personal statement** about how your passion for your subject of choice developed and what your goals are. The statement is usually a summary of your life path.

In writing your personal statement, think about what has influenced your choices. You may want or need to share the story of obstacles you have overcome, ranging from living on welfare to being ill to parental death. I have known program participants who have surmounted physical deformity, a parent with a terminal illness, recent migration from a war-torn nation, and homelessness. Obviously, trauma is not required, but sometimes it is part of what makes you who you are, and it speaks of your resilience and perhaps the source of your passion.

Take the personal statement seriously, as it is a window into who you are. Be sure to have several trusted persons read it, and do more than one draft (probably several), as this is a hugely important ingredient in the pursuit of competitive honors and awards.

Similarly, prepare yourself for interviews. They may be required with key faculty or administrators or even peers currently in the program. You can ask for mock interviews to help you work out nervousness and quirks, such as twirling your hair or not making eye contact. Be knowledgeable about your field and where it fits into the global picture. Read newspapers and newsmagazines to know what is most current about your interest within the larger scheme of things. If you're a biologist, what do you know about the current stem cell debate? If you're an English major, what do you think about the most recent Pulitzer Prize fiction winner?

Letters of recommendation are also required, and you can learn more about how to ask your professors for them in chapter 5, The Professors. Most important is to ask them well enough in advance that they can prepare and do a good job for you. Remember, they love helping wonderful students— someone once did it for them.

Schools also offer **honors programs or honors colleges** that you should explore if you are a good student. In some cases, you apply for and enter such programs as freshmen, in others you become eligible once in college. They give you access to additional attention from professors and special chances to do research and expand the range of options for your own work. They may stretch you intellectually and in exciting ways. Your advisors can tell you more, and if you're showing promise they may approach you about these opportunities.

Almost all schools have a **dean's list** for students who achieve a high grade point average consistently (usually without pass/fail or withdrawals). The dean's list always looks great on a résumé—make it a goal. Rules vary from campus to campus, and you should check your campus rules in the catalog or with an advisor.

Along the way, and especially as you enter your junior year, you will begin to hear about **special fellowships and postgraduate opportunities**. One of the most well known of these is the Rhodes Scholarship program (President Bill Clinton was a Rhodes Scholar), but the Marshall, Fulbright, Gates, and others are all highly prestigious and geared to the very best students with GPAs at the 3.8 level or above. These students also have résumés that reflect several leadership positions, a passion for a subject, and a record of overcoming tough obstacles. The reward is study abroad, perhaps at Oxford or Cambridge in England, and extraordinarily high regard that remains through your whole life.

The fellowships are worth the work that goes into the application process. Talk to the dean or advisor who oversees these and other such awards. Some, such as the Goldwater (sciences) or the Truman (public service), require applications in the junior year. Again, see an advisor for details of your campus's processes. If you have the grades and the range of experiences, count yourself in rather than out. Go for the gold.

Finally, awards that honor sheer student excellence include the **Phi Beta Kappa**, the national honor society for many of the nation's best students (chapters exist on only 256 campuses). Various subject areas have their own honor societies, such as Pi Mu Epsilon in mathematics, for which your department may nominate you. And at graduation you may qualify for what are called **Latin honors**, classifications on your diploma of *summa cum laude* (with highest honors), *magna cum laude* (with high honors), or *cum laude* (with honors). Each school has its own GPA designation for each of these levels, and they are worth striving for. Departments also have honors programs that may require a special research paper and/or seminar; these are for the top students in a major. It never hurts to be able to say that you graduated with honors.

All of these honors should go on your résumé and help you stand out in the early stages of building your career. Remember, being smart is what gets you ahead professionally, and all of these awards, honors, and experiences are evidence that you are among the best!

A Story: Enrique

Enrique was the first in his family to go to college. He envisioned pursuing a career in physical therapy, because he knew how useful it had been to his mother. He had also heard that it was a secure career.

He attended a public college, and in one of his psychology classes a professor spotted his talent in the lab. When the director of the McNair Program (aimed at providing mentored research opportunities to college students from underrepresented populations) was seeking recommendations for the program, this professor pushed Enrique to apply. He did, going through a process requiring a personal statement and an interview.

On acceptance he was given a chance to work with a professor who mentored him and taught him more about lab work. Enrique got to make presentations at conferences about the research he was doing. Then his mentor encouraged him to apply to the Summer Program for Undergraduate Research (SPUR) at a prestigious local university, where he learned even more about the world of scientific and medical research. He gained self-confidence and by his senior year he saw himself as a potential scholar.

Now he is in a doctoral program, where the research he does may help far more people than he could have done as a physical therapist.

Your choice of courses and majors will be critical. You need to select ones that will engage you and show what you are capable of. Their subject matter may not connect to the careers you may have over a lifetime, but they will build the skills you need. If done with a focus on your interests and strengths, then you have the chance to scale the heights to honors and new challenging experiences. These will be the gateway to the life of success you are seeking from your college degree.

Chapter 5
THE PROFESSORS

Many students are intimidated by the teachers who stand in front of the classroom presenting volumes of material that they then expect you to know. True, they *do* have power—they grade your work after all. But they have also all been in your shoes. Most college teachers are in the classroom because they love the subject they teach and enjoy sharing it with individuals like you. This is a calling—work done more for passion than glory—and few can get rich doing it. What gives them pleasure is the student who also loves the subject area or who makes a real effort to understand and appreciate it. So when professors tell you to visit them during office hours, you should do it. Whether you want to continue discussion of a point raised in class, learn more about an area, or seek advice about how to do better, they welcome your interest and initiative.

Remember that the research a professor does begins with a question. They have a problem they want to solve or question they want to answer. Therefore they begin with inquiry. They understand and relate to those who also engage in asking questions. When you ask a question of a professor you are speaking their language. This is a good and not a bad thing. You want to be recognized as curious and interested.

At some point the professors you engage with may write your recommendations for graduate schools, fellowships, awards, and even jobs. They may become mentors for your own research work.

A Story: Ginny

Ginny had gotten a C– on her midterm paper. She had been diligent about attending class and had done the readings, but she panicked because she didn't know how to write a paper. First she was angry and blamed the professor. Then she was depressed and got drunk. Finally she went to the professor and asked why she had gotten the C–, her lowest grade ever.

The professor taught her how to organize a paper and then offered to work with her as she prepared the final one. Ginny got early approval of her topic, did an outline, and discussed it with the professor. She also asked for a critique on a rough draft. Her final product was an A– paper. Later, when Ginny was applying for a fellowship, she asked her teacher for a letter of recommendation. The professor was happy to talk about Ginny's work ethic and determination to learn. Ginny won the fellowship.

Be respectful of instructors' time, as they are busy. Outside of office hours, make appointments or at least call ahead, rather than dropping in. Office hours are usually announced at the beginning of a course or on the professor's door or website.

Even if you're taking courses online you should develop ties to the faculty teaching them, whether by email, chat room, or Skype. If you're an older student you may even have a basis for a closer rapport with your professors. Over time they may turn out to be your friends and real influences in your life.

A Story: Peter Bachrach

Peter Bachrach taught political science in the 1960s at Bryn Mawr College in Pennsylvania. Not long ago, when he was in his nineties, he died. His widow was overwhelmed by letters and memorials from his former students, all of whom had been greatly influenced in their work, careers, and scholarship by his teaching and connections with the former students.

The faculty have worked hard to get where they are. This is a career or a calling for them. They thrive on learning more and sharing what they have learned.

Most often the faculty's training has taken them at least to the master's degree level, especially if the MA is the highest degree attainable in their field, such as the master's in fine arts. In four-year colleges, you usually encounter faculty who have earned the PhD, which means they are considered expert in their field. They commonly study for six years and produce a body of work called a dissertation, which reflects some new knowledge or perspective that they've been able to bring to their chosen field. They have read hundreds of books and often written dozens of papers, as well as books of their own.

You may be taught by graduate students who are training to become professors, but who are already experts in their fields even if they haven't quite completed the degree required. You may also be taught by faculty called **adjuncts** who may or may not have a doctorate, but who may bring specialized expertise and/or experience from the work world. They may not be full time at your school and may teach at other colleges too. Some are called clinical professors because they have significant practical expertise based on current real-world experience that makes them as expert as any PhD. They may be practicing MDs or corporate senior executives, for example.

Full-time faculty members are ranked by their experience and their scholarly contributions. Full professors are at the top of the heap and lecturers (often adjuncts) at the lower end, with (in descending order) associate and assistant professor and instructor titles in between. Full professors have done the most work in a field, contributing greatly to the body of knowledge and to the institutions where they teach. All who are in front of the class, however, bring something special to your learning experience.

At universities emphasizing research, faculty members are expected to produce books, articles, and presentations that bring their work to the attention of other scholars and add to the body of knowledge. These works are often put through a rigorous process of review by peer scholars who validate or critique the theories put forth. In addition, at any school, faculty must prepare to teach their classes.

All of these activities and obligations are obviously time-consuming—the actual time in front of a class is but a small fraction of it. These professors must prepare every lecture, map out exercises, and review materials (perhaps for the hundredth time!). Instructors teaching a new course can spend easily more than thirteen hours per lecture or class period preparing. And they have to grade any work they've assigned. I've often wondered what I was thinking when I assigned a twenty-page final paper to a class of twenty students—that totals four hundred pages of reading I had to do by the time grades were due.

If professors are teaching three courses in a semester and have assigned papers and/or finals for each, they typically have only a short time to review the work and submit grades. Yet, thoughtful instructors take the time to offer suggestions and corrections on papers and exams, so that students can learn from the experience and enhance their work the next time around.

Professors must also serve on various committees and engage in other work that helps keep the school functioning. Those who do all of these things well are granted tenure (lifetime employment) through a tough process that takes years of vetting by peers.

STUDENT-FACULTY INTERACTIONS

What can you expect from faculty members? You will connect with some better than others. Some will have a teaching style that matches your learning style well. Some will be more entertaining than others. No matter—teacher and student on every campus, real-world or virtual, should have a certain set of expectations of one another that are plainly set out.

You teacher should provide a clear roadmap to the course, otherwise known as a **syllabus**. It tells you what the course is about; the assignments on a class-by-class basis; the general expectations; how, where, and when you can find your professor; how grades are determined; and if there are optional tasks or resources you can engage. The grading policy should be clearly laid out. You should know, for example, if grading is on a curve (when the class's top score is considered an A and the rest align accordingly) or if points are deducted for absences. (It is possible to fail a course based on absences alone, since the instructor may assume you cannot absorb the material if you're not present.) Books should be ordered and available in the bookstore or library. Material should be clear and coherent.

Both you and the professor should come to class prepared, she or he with a lecture or class plan and you with readings or assignments done. Courtesy is a two-way street—you and the professor have an obligation to each other and to the other students to be polite and respectful. You may disagree with a point of view offered in class, but do so politely, using thoughtful evidence, not just your gut feeling. Remember, the instructor has done the research, and while there can be more than one side to an issue, both sides should be supported by facts. So if you disagree, do not be surprised by the question, "And why have you reached that conclusion…?"

Info: Class-y Behavior

During class, do not

- a) beat out a cadence on your desk while the teacher is lecturing
- b) sigh audibly more than three or four times during a class period
- c) check your watch more than twice during the hour

Do not ask any of the following:

"Will this be on the test?"

"Does grammar count?"

"Do we have to read the whole chapter?"

"Can I turn my paper in late?"

—*Professor Carol Berkin,* New York Times, *September 6, 2009*

Overt rudeness is never a good strategy. You never know when you might need the professor whom you have "dissed" for a letter of recommendation one day. So do not walk out of class, call names, eat (unless you're told it's okay), come late frequently, not come at all with no excuse, turn in work late, use your cell phone, send email, text friends, or sleep in class.

Disagreements and Disputes

What if you do disagree, for example, on **your grade** (the most frequent source of dispute between students and faculty)? First you need to be sure you understand the basis of the grade. Recheck the syllabus to see how the grades are determined. Most often some percentage of a grade is derived from exams, quizzes, midterms, and/or finals—all are ways of measuring how well you have absorbed and understood the material. Papers or projects are other factors. Class participation often counts, especially in small classes where discussion is a key element of the learning process. But look for how these are weighted. If participation counts for 25 percent of the grade and you're absent a lot and sleep in class the rest of the time, then don't expect many points in that category. (These factors alone can drop your grade to a B, even before you've taken a test or done a paper.)

If your paper is supposed to be ten pages long and you turn in seven pages, double space in fourteen-point type, you're not going to get an A. If it's a research paper, then citing Wikipedia does not count. Good grades are about not only doing the work, but doing it well. It's about quality—your work should be grammatical, logical, aligned with instructions, and thoughtful, as a bare minimum.

So if you're struggling to understand the lecture, doing badly on quizzes, or seeing lots of red marks on your midterm paper, then you need to go see your professor to ask what you're doing wrong and how to improve. In grading in non-quantitative courses, a subjective factor often exists, and the sincerity of your effort could be the difference between a B and a B+. High grades are not an entitlement because you pay the bills and deign to attend class—they are a reflection of real effort and energy.

If you've been to the professor, however, and she will not budge or cannot be found (which sometimes happens with part-time faculty), then go to the **department chair**, the boss of the department where the instructor teaches. This is the person who can locate a wayward professor, seek evidence of why a grade was given, and help negotiate an understanding and an amicable resolution. Do not try to go above this person; you'll get marked as a troublemaker if you write to the president of the college and copy the board of trustees about your grade—this approach does not make friends. Furthermore, these officials are not empowered to change grades; that is the purview of the faculty.

With a disputed grade, you may be in a good position to make your case, if you've kept copies of emails and all assignments, graded papers, and exams. To prove that you turned in a paper on a specific date, for example, you may need a computer record. Keep *everything* until you have your diploma in hand.

What to do in cases where an instructor may not be performing well—if students feel that a professor seems disorganized, is often late or absent, or is difficult to understand? If there is collective agreement among you and your classmates that a professor presents issues that are truly standing in the way of learning, then as a group you can approach the department chair. You need to have evidence—the situation cannot be about personalities or politics or personal disputes, but clearly identifiable issues preventing learning. The chair may have heard the complaint before or may then have the professor observed in class. There is never any guarantee of a change—especially if the professor has tenure or has been at the school for a long time. But it is better to raise the issue in a collective and objective way than to let it persist to your detriment.

If your dispute is not about pedagogy but is personal—a comment you feel is racist, a case of sexual harassment, of personal disrespect—there are other procedures to follow. Every school has a policy and protocol regarding sexual harassment charges, usually spelled out in the catalog and/or on the website. In such a case, do *not* go to the department chair, but to whatever person or office is designated for that protocol. It may be appropriate at your school to go to either a dean or, if your campus has one, an **ombudsman** (a school official trained in dispute resolution) to solve a personal issue that seems intractable.

One dispute you may find yourself in with a professor is the charge of **plagiarism**. First you need to understand what plagiarism is: basically, it is theft. When you quote or use someone else's ideas as your own, without permission or without citing the source, you are essentially stealing their ideas, and you are cheating by using them as your own. You would be pretty annoyed if you wrote a story and found out that another student had won an award for publishing it as his own—he stole your work! Well, it's the same effect when you do not use quotation marks, footnotes, parenthetical citations, or other techniques that give credit to the originator of the work you are using.

You can find **style manuals or guides**, which explain the right way to cite your sources, online and in the library or bookstore. There are variations from field to field, so if your professor does not tell you, ask which style is preferred.

Info: Style Guides

To address the myriad style issues that come up when you're writing papers, a few common guides can answer your questions. The Modern Language Association issues the MLA guide, which applies generally to the humanities courses (literature, English and other languages, philosophy, music, and the arts). The social sciences (psychology, sociology, economics, anthropology, archeology, history, political science) tend to use the rules of the American Psychological Association, or APA guide. The sciences (biology, chemistry, physics, engineering, and their subsets) may prefer the Council of Science Editors, or CSE style.

If you do plagiarize and get caught, you can suffer penalties ranging from failing the class to getting thrown out of school. The theft of ideas in an academic context is taken *very* seriously. Neither is worth it in the long run. Turnitin, the Web-based tool that faculty now use to scan for duplication, among others things, makes it possible for instructors to find out in seconds if you have plagiarized. Every college has a plagiarism policy—become familiar with your school's. The consequences can damage your career. If you're applying to law school, for example, and your college has to attest to your integrity, they cannot if there is a record of your having cheated in any way. No form of cheating is permitted.

A Cautionary Tale: Cheating

Two friends who were just finishing their junior year and had excellent records of success in and out of the classroom decided to study for a biology exam together. They exchanged information with each other via email. Their professor had told the class not to collaborate on the exam, and so when the two friends had the same wrong answers, he knew that they had been sharing information. Further, their communication was traceable on their computers. The college's honor board determined that they had cheated and suspended them for a term, thus delaying their graduation and tarnishing what would otherwise have been stellar records.

Lessons learned: Don't cheat. Be aware of the rules as laid out by both the school and in each class. Take no chances—behave ethically.

If you do have a dispute about cheating or plagiarism, where you are being accused of it but don't believe you are guilty, be sure to have verifiable evidence of your integrity. Such charges are unpleasant and produce a lot of work in many quarters. They are not levied lightly. If you are charged, it is serious, and you need to defend yourself rigorously if you believe you are innocent and support it with evidence. You should be able to show that what you have said is not a direct lift from another source. (One student was able to show that he had done significant research in the area and was therefore able to paraphrase sources based on his knowledge of the field.) But you are always on safer ground if you cite, even parenthetically, sources you are using. These charges are very hard to defend and the F (or worse) you may get is not worth the time saved by not making that extra effort.

The Positive Side

On the other hand, 90 percent of your experiences with your professors can and should be positive. These teachers can be your best advocates. They are the ones who notice that you have talents you yourself may not have recognized. They may spot a problem just because you were unusually quiet in class. They can even become your friends as years go by (most of my Facebook friends are former students).

One of the most important roles professors can play, once you have established a good rapport, is to write **letters of recommendation** for you for special programs, academic scholarships, graduate schools, postgraduate fellowships, and even jobs, as pointed out earlier. If you think this is a bother for them, remember that, first, someone did the same for them and that, second, it is part of their job. As a professor, it is also a pleasure to be able to say good things about a student you have come to know and value.

That said, you should observe certain courtesies when asking for these letters. First, plan well ahead so that you are not asking for a letter a couple of days before it is due. Give plenty of time—two weeks or more is best—perhaps even longer if it is needed at a busy time or right after the summer break. Also ask whether your professor agrees to write a recommendation for you. It could happen, for example, that two people have asked him for letters for the same program, which could be awkward.

With a yes in hand, provide your professor with ample information:

- a pleasant letter in which you remind him of your ties: the courses you took with him, your grades, or papers you wrote
- a description of the grant, program, or school you're applying for or to
- a copy of your résumé
- a rough draft of your application or personal statement
- any forms she has to sign or fill out (you may have to fill in some part of these yourself)
- envelopes that are already stamped and addressed if she has to mail something

In my experience, it has worked well when students who needed several letters from me for various graduate programs gave me a cover sheet with timelines and key information, to make the process as clear as possible. When that happened, I was impressed and even more convinced that these students were mature, thoughtful, and well organized—good qualities for graduate students.

After your supporters write these letters, which do require thought and effort, be sure to not only say thank-you, but more important, tell them what happens. Let them know when you are accepted or what your ultimate career or postgraduate plans are. They want to know the outcome of their efforts and celebrate with you. This can be one of the most joyful parts of the job for them.

It's necessary here to say something about the difference between **mentorship** and friendship. Faculty members with whom you have a good relationship of mutual respect may be helping to guide you along the college path and even beyond, especially if you are continuing in the same field—this can be considered a mentoring relationship. It may be formalized if you're doing research, for example, on a project the professor is working on, or if she or he is overseeing some of your own work as part of a formal program such as the NIMH/COR fellowship in social sciences (the National Institute of Mental Health–Career Opportunities in Research Program). This mentoring role may even continue later when you seek guidance on graduate school or career choices from a respected faculty member who has come to know you well.

On the contrary, your instructors are not, and should not be, your drinking buddies, surrogate parents, or marriage counselors. They should never be dates (they can be fired for that). Remember, they're in the position of grading your efforts and writing recommendations for you—you always want to be seen in the best light in their eyes. It's best to keep things on a friendly but professional level. Later in life you may come to know them as peers or even colleagues, and the barriers can then shift as appropriate.

Another group you encounter who are in a somewhat ambiguous, but also helpful and important, role are **graduate students**. They are usually working toward a doctoral degree and may be engaged as **teaching assistants** (TAs) or even instructors/adjunct professors in their fields. They may also serve as advisors or in other roles on campus. Such jobs help to pay for their education, but, as we mentioned earlier, they are also learning to be professors and sometimes administrators as they go. Because they are closer in age to you, in most cases, they may relate more directly to what you're dealing with and can be easier to talk to.

In large lecture classes, often taught by a senior professor, graduate students teach or lead small-group sessions that accompany the lecture. They may be called **recitation, discussion, or seminar sessions** (or other names on different campuses). These sessions allow for questions and discussion and provide a great place to check that you really know what is going on and to get help if you need it. The grad students, as teaching assistants, often do the grading or assist in the process. In a lab setting they may lead activities for undergraduates as well. They function as apprentices to the faculty, learning the craft by doing it. This being said, they deserve to be treated with the same respect and cautions as the full faculty.

There are many different sorts of individuals and college officials who play many kinds of roles in your progression through school. The faculty is one of many who are part of your team.

Chapter 6
YOUR PEOPLE

There was an H & R Block commercial in which characters say they have "people" who take care of their financial needs, and a Verizon ad featured a herd of folks who followed around each customer, supporting his or her every communications need. At college you too have "people."

There are lots of people who play varying roles for you in college, some constructive and some not so. They range from your roommate(s) to your deans. In between are teachers, advisors, counselors, coaches, employers, family members, and even ancestors. Most have your best interests at heart, even if it does not always feel that way. Yet, though all have the same stated interest in your well-being, they may not be in agreement. In some cases, parental desires conflict with college policy, fraternity demands conflict with a professor's demands, a professor's priorities conflict with your coach's, your girlfriend's plans don't mesh with your need to be at a job, and none fit with your need for sleep. Thus it is important to understand, set priorities, and align the roles that all your people play in your college success.

A Story: Daniella

Daniella came from an old Eastern European family with a long-standing family business. Her family sent her to college in the States with the express intention of preparing her to return home, marry the man of their choice, and run the family business. They even specified what her major should be (economics).

She got to college and fell in love with a young man unknown to her family. She had also fallen in love with the field of psychology, also unknown to her family. As soon as she took her first economics course, she knew that major would not be right for her, and she fought with her father all the time. But she still felt she had to do what the family expected, at least in her career.

In her sophomore year, Daniella heard a dean speak on recognizing one's own strengths and following one's passions. She decided to meet with that dean and explain her quandary. The dean agreed to talk to Daniella's father about the change of major to psychology, explaining to him how important understanding human behavior would be to the family firm's marketing and human relations. The dean also pointed out to Daniella's father that he would be able to keep his daughter's love and end the arguments that were part of all their conversations.

This college official became one of the individuals Daniella sought out for all sorts of advice, and her family felt that, even far away from home, she was in sensible hands. The dean was one of Daniella's people.

The reality is that you need people, your people, your posse. Some years ago, a study noted that those with the biggest contact lists also had the biggest bank accounts and were the most at ease in moving professionally—all because they had wide-ranging contacts.

When you ask someone high ranking how they got there, they cite someone along the way who made a difference in their life. In a recent conversation with a group of students, I asked them which person was the key motivator in their lives, and responses ranged from mothers and fathers to grandparents, a prison warden, a social worker, an employer, a professor, a coach, spouses, and even children.

But beyond this group of people who are close to you, you need your own "board of directors"—individuals whom you can turn to for guidance and good counsel. Though they may not always say what you *want* to hear, they may be telling you what you *need* to hear.

College is a good place to widen your range of contacts and your support team. It's where you begin to build the networks and relationships that can provide sounding boards and access to new opportunities and ways of seeing things. It is no accident that Facebook began on a campus and that LinkedIn uses colleges as a key basis for connections. College is a basic social network.

Students sometimes feel they have to go it alone to prove themselves. That is not, however, the way the world works. Sports and work both require teamwork, and families are social units. We are not cut out to be alone. Isolated individuals are more likely to be depressed, ill, and lacking in the skills that lead to success.

The best students study in groups or seek tutors. They ask other students, faculty, advisors, or mentors for help. When you don't know, you're more likely to get answers from someone else who has experience than from your own head. Learning how to tap into and use your human resources is another life lesson you acquire in college.

One way to get more comfortable with this idea is to remember that it is a reciprocal process. For every person who helps you along the way, there is someone else who needs something you have to offer and whom you can help. Sometimes it will be the same person. Say you're good at math but not at writing papers, and your friend is just the opposite. As adding peanut butter to chocolate produces a win-win result, so does this kind of reciprocity.

Sometimes this may occur over time—the person you help out now may be able to help you later. *Good Morning America* once did a segment on individuals who had affected someone else's life. One story was of a young man who invited a fellow student, who saw herself as unpopular, to a party with the popular kids on campus. She had been ready to leave school (or worse), and his one act of kindness transformed her feelings of inadequacy and her life. Twenty years later she thanked him on national television.

You never know which interactions may have far-reaching effects. Don't forget, you have people! Some of the most influential and important are right in front of you. Among your people, your family is going to be a central force in your life.

FAMILY

Your family has been concerned about you and your future during the course of your lifetime, and they certainly are now that you're in college. They are seeking a good outcome—they want to assure that you'll be happy, employed or employable, well grounded, well regarded, and well educated.

They may go farther. They may have particular career plans for you or may envision your education completed in time for you to give them grandchildren when you're twenty-five. If you're not yet married, they may have their own view of who your mate should be or look like. They may expect you to follow in their footsteps in the family business. Your parents, spouse, aunts, or uncles may expect you to succeed in college and at the same time take care of siblings or grandparents, or work at the family store. And they feel that all of these expectations are reasonable and in your interest.

You may begin college fully understanding and embracing these desires too. But college can, should, and will change your worldview. You may discover new talents or interests, ones that can lead to great success and happiness but are not what your family envisioned. You may meet persons of different faiths, nationalities, and races and make friends and perhaps choose life partners as a result. You may discover that your career path of choice— the MD or PhD, for instance—will take many years of work and study, which could delay the grandkids a bit longer than your parents thought. You may find that your love of art history should take you to France for a term, making care for siblings difficult. Your family may think you should major in economics for a business career, but you have learned (even from this book) that you can get there by another path such as psychology. Sadly, I have seen good intentions cause real pain to students who want to make their families happy, but also need to follow their own paths to fulfillment.

Here is the trick to managing the tricky relationship with your family's expectations. First, accept that your family wants the best. Then, as you evolve into new interests and relationships, share what you're learning and thinking and how it's working to your benefit. Let them know the good grades you're getting in your new major, and tell them about the good things professors are saying about your work. Tell them about the successful alumna you heard speak about her career path. When they're on campus, be sure to introduce them to a range of your friends and professors.

Part of my job as a dean was to help students frame strategies for dealing with difficult family communication. I've advised students, for instance, to tell parents they planned to be corporate executives, even though they really didn't know yet what they wanted to do. But they needed an answer to the question at Thanksgiving, "What are you going to be when you finish?" This answer bought the students time and sounds prestigious. Some students did in fact become corporate executives! Others became professors or social workers, or took up other good and worthwhile careers.

A Story: Maria

Maria, whose family came from Bolivia, was the oldest child and the first to go to college. In Maria's psychology class at her city college, a professor presented some of her research on children and speech, and Maria was fascinated. She sought out the professor, and they spent time discussing the project. The professor suggested that Maria apply for a special program, leading ultimately to a doctorate, that would provide a stipend and also allow her to work formally with this same faculty member. Maria was accepted into the program, which put her on a career path very different from the one her parents had envisioned (teaching elementary school).

In time she was also offered a chance to take part in a summer research program in the Midwest, far from home. Her parents were frightened that she would be far away and unable to take care of her little sisters at home. But Maria and her advisor explained to the parents that the program was prestigious and Maria was special to be selected.

Maria's summer away from home enabled her parents to get used to her absence, and they were proud of her achievement. They became even prouder when, after being selected for both the research and summer programs as a result of her higher visibility with college officials, Maria was often asked to speak publicly.

By the time Maria left home to go away to graduate school, where she is earning her doctorate, her parents had had time to adjust to the new goals and the new person their daughter was becoming.

A Story: Bob

Bob's dad was a prominent lawyer who expected his son to someday join the firm. Bob, however, was interested in and talented at making movies. He took every chance he had in college to make films, to video events, and to build his skills. He sought summer internships in the industry and made contacts. After college, he took an intensive film course and then went West. In L.A. he did the dirty work around the studios and finally got noticed. His father is now proud to see his son's name in the credits of a major TV show.

Some parents can be quite strict, again out of good intentions and hopes of sparing their children suffering that they themselves have experienced. It is a protective impulse. It may also be a product of a culture that is less permissive than is typical in the United States. Now permissiveness creates its own problems, but students often find it more difficult to be more restricted.

I have known students whose parents expected them home within a half-hour of their last class of the day. Not only does this limit the student's social life with peers, it also means not being able to engage in the all-important résumé-building activities of late-afternoon or evening campus clubs and activities. It's important for families to understand how these activities help get you to the goal you're seeking. You may want to bring home new friends so your family can see that they share admirable values. You may want to ask a dean or advisor to speak to a parent about the role that extracurricular activities play in students' lives. Visiting on a parents' weekend can help (if it is not a party weekend too!). Showing that you understand parental fears and are responsible is the best strategy. Good grades can prove the point perhaps better than anything.

Families can also have trouble adjusting to the new friends you may make, especially ones of differing backgrounds. My first college roommate—in the 1960s—was a white coed from Mississippi and her family was unhappy to have her rooming with a Black girl. But we really clicked and became great friends. By the time we graduated, and once they got to know me and my family, her parents had adjusted. But it was not easy getting there.

Interracial, interfaith, or gay/lesbian relationships—even relationships that cross class lines—can unsettle families. Taking new friends home with you or asking them to join you for dinner on parents' weekend can help your family adjust.

Sometimes you might be the one feeling uncomfortable. Colleges are diverse places, and you'll meet different people at meals, in classes, on projects, on teams, in clubs, and at parties. This is part of your preparation to engage in a diverse world. If you find any such issues challenging, discuss them with someone who can be helpful. Campus advisors or counselors, clubs, or programs can likely help with adjustment issues—in, for example, an Office of Diversity or a GLBT center or chaplain's office.

A Story: Troy

By his junior year Troy had come to accept and appreciate the fact that he was gay. He became sufficiently comfortable with this realization—and with his ability to celebrate the freedom of being who he truly was—that he told his parents over a holiday weekend. They did not respond well and fought among themselves, using him as the reason. He began to feel enormous guilt and to experience depression. Over time he started to act out in ways that put him at risk. Finally he broke down in a dean's office.

She helped him see that his parents' problems were present before his announcement and guided him to campus resources where he could comfortably discuss his situation. Troy started to emerge as a real leader and ultimately went on to business school and a life of his own choosing. In time, his family reconciled to his new identity and accepted the successful young man he had become.

You may also find yourself having trouble adjusting to being away from the family environment you are used to. You may feel comfortable, safe, and cared for at home. Mom or Nana cooks the meals and no one can do your favorite dishes like they can. But now, you are expected to take care of everything for yourself.

One of the most surprising challenges for students away from home for the first time is the need to do their own laundry. Clean clothes do not appear magically week after week. I knew one young man who when at Yale would go home to the Bronx on the weekend taking his laundry to his mom! A key aspect of the college experience is to become self-sufficient in all respects. Becoming familiar with a container of Tide, or how to wash pots and pans, is all part of that process.

An Open Letter to Families

Sometimes it is hard to say what you need to say to family members and it is easier if the message comes from a person that could be acknowledged as trustworthy. I hope that I can be that person and so offer this letter for you to share with your family about the college experience and what they might expect.

Dear Parent, Spouse, Sister, Brother, Aunt, or Uncle,

Your loved one is about to embark on an adventure that you all have helped to make possible. You want the best for him or her. You want the success of college to lead to success in life. That is what we all want. And we want to help you appreciate aspects of this new world your student is becoming part of, so you can be supportive in the best ways.

One thing you will find is that college is designed to open the minds of its students, exposing them to new ideas, individuals, and opportunities. So your student may begin with one plan or career path, but become aware of different interests and strengths that he can use to pursue exciting new ventures. Professors may see talents that you or your student did not know she had.

College students are learning to think more independently and to examine and challenge everything, from what they see on TV to what they have believed for a lifetime. This shows growth and is actually a goal of a college education. Students are expected to become inquiring thinkers. Employers seek this attribute.

Career paths are created on good grades, full records of achievement, and compelling résumés—not based on a particular set of courses. You do not have to major in biology to be a doctor nor in political science to be a lawyer.

College requires time, focus, and dedication, and will probably take away from time spent in the past on family obligations. Building a résumé demands extracurricular college activities, which take more time, but which build essential networks and leadership skills. It is a bonus if your student is asked to travel for research or as a leadership activity. The investment of time now will result later in a greatly enriched future.

As my late mother-in-law used to say, "You have to hold on to your children with open hands." Talk to your school's dean about how it all works and what you can do to better understand students' experiences. Attend any orientations or parent events. Be there for awards or honors of any kind. Cheer on your students for their achievements. They will do you proud.

One of the things that families find frustrating is that they are not in a position to see or know all that is going on in your life while you are at school. But family members are not privy to all aspects of your college experience. This is part of the transition to full adulthood for the traditional student entering college at eighteen.

You should know, for example, that parents or others, even if paying the bills, are not entitled to your grades or any information about your life on campus, unless you give permission or there is a life-threatening circumstance. One of the protections you have as a student is the **Buckley Amendment (FERPA, the Family Educational Rights and Privacy Act)**, which stipulates such privacy protection while you're in school. There were many times in my life as a dean when I had information about a student that, as a parent, I would have wanted to know, but I could not reveal it to family members. My job was to encourage students to share necessary information with their families while trying to ensure that they got whatever support or aid they needed.

But it will ultimately be your choice what to share with your parents. As we've said earlier, college is a transitional time when you are expected to take more responsibility for yourself and the consequences of your actions. Thus, grades earned or experiences had, whether good or bad, are yours to own.

This is your time to emerge from the family unit as a whole person with your own skills, strengths, choices, and even frailties.

FRIENDS

Friends are wonderful and essential, but they can also be distracting and even mislead you. They may have your best interests in mind, or sometimes they may have their own. I would say that the friend who suggests you, as an underage person, buy the keg does not have your best interests in mind. But the friend who puts you to bed when you've been up studying for thirty-six hours—instead of suggesting you party—does have your best interests in mind, even if in the moment you would rather party.

As you know from high school and earlier, those you call your friends can be a transient grouping. In fact, among the most fragile relationships you may have during your time in college can be the ones from high school and home.

Once you're in school and not spending time with your old friends, you begin to change. And if they've stayed behind or gone elsewhere, they are changing too. You're no longer sharing experiences that come with being in the same homeroom or neighborhood or basketball court. You—and they—may be doing new things, and you're not paramount in each others' minds anymore. You may be able to manage this easily with some of your old friends, less so with others.

At first this can feel awkward or even painful. The old ties just won't fit the same way anymore. You may need to spend more time on campus and less at home, and you may be connecting through campus clubs with students whose backgrounds are similar, but whose current experience more closely mirrors your own. And if you're a commuter student, you may find that your friends who have not gone to college may even resent your moving on and may dismiss you or try to undermine your efforts by luring you out when you need to study, and this can be difficult to handle. Moving apart from old friends is never easy, but know that it is natural. The most important thing is not to let it derail you from achieving your goal of graduating college—that is the most important thing.

The good news is that, even if the circumstances today find you moving apart from your high school friends, you may find each other again much later. Thirty years after separating from each other for college and marriages and other life experiences, my high school best friend and I have reconnected. We see each other a few times a year and now have brought in others from our high school class too.

A rule of thumb for all friendships is reciprocity—you both care no matter if circumstances are up or down; you both give and take without imbalance on one side or the other; you don't get each other in trouble or hide troubles that need outside help. The friendship helps each of you feel good and be your best self. Watch out for users who want to be around you for what you can do for them. Beware too of those who expect you to be their cheerleader, but won't do the same for you.

That sounds like a tall order. But how do you begin to make these kinds of friends in a whole new environment?

So the big question is, How do you make friends in college? If you're in a residential college, you've likely been paired with a **roommate** (or a few). If you're lucky, you mesh—it does happen. My mother was best friends with her college roommate for sixty years. At the very least, a roommate may be someone to hang with while you both find your way around.

In fact, colleges work hard to pair roommates that they hope will be compatible, by offering questionnaires to root out upfront some of the major causes of friction between potential roommates, such as disharmony in lifestyle and taste preferences—including eating, drinking, night-owl vs. early-riser habits, music styles, etc.

No matter what the situation with your roommate, the key to living together will be trust. Even if you hit it off perfectly with your roommate, you should have some rules about the sharing of your space and belongings. My son and his roommates were the same size and wore one another's clothes—by mutual agreement, not "borrowing" without consent. Doing that would have been a breach of trust. Trust also means you do not share confidences or items considered private with anyone outside the room unless you're clear it's okay to do so. Mutual respect is key when you're living in close quarters with someone.

It may, however, turn out that you and your roommate are polar opposites. She is a Republican who goes to church every Sunday and thinks beer is nasty; you're a Democrat verging on radical, have not seen a church since your baptism, and think college is a party. You can still survive, if you are respectful.

But if your situation is really untenable, then go to your **residence advisor (RA)** and begin a conversation about making a change. If that's not immediately possible, then wait for the second semester, when some students may leave their rooms, freeing up space. Or seek a single or a suite with like-minded classmates for the next year. If things are really ugly, seek counseling for both of you to work out terms for coexistence for the semester. Ninety-five percent of the time, things will be just fine.

Outside of your room, all the other persons on campus await. A joy of college life on a campus, whether residential or not, can be the long conversations with other students about life, philosophy, politics, professors, dating, music, books, families, food. You can lose as much sleep talking as doing anything else late at night (like studying). You may meet these new friends in lounges or study rooms, cafeterias or coffee shops, clubrooms or campus hang-out spaces. You too may find lifelong friends. And sometimes they are the individuals you least expect.

A Story: Riva

Riva had been raised as an Orthodox Jew in New York City. She had no exposure to anyone of another faith and little to individuals of other cultures. At college she found herself on a campus with all kinds of students, including Muslims, about whom she had numerous preconceived ideas. She began to see that, counter to her beliefs, they

were as devoted to their families and their faith, and to learning and
service, as she was. As she did, they also shared an avoidance of
pork as part of their religious practice. Some even shared her love of
European classical music and of dancing. Riva began to make a variety
of friends and to engage in campus projects to bring diverse groups
together. Ultimately that became her passion and her life's work.

Another way to make new friends is through shared interests found in
clubs and organizations. These have the added value of being a place to
show the talents you may develop in your professional life. The woman who
directed our class play in college has been a world renowned theater director
ever since.

While I do not suggest that you load up on a bunch of clubs or activities
in your first term while you're getting your footing, it is a good idea to join
something. There may be clubs that relate to your religion or ethnicity or
country of origin that can feel comfortable and provide support while you
settle in. You may veer from them later, but they can ground you at first. Or
you may end up taking on a leadership role in one over time. If you were on
the high school newspaper, then you may want to work on the college paper.
If you're musical, then a band or orchestra might be a good choice. One
young man who had never played an instrument learned to play the tuba in
the college marching band, which provided the structure he needed to succeed. There are usually hundreds of options. Sometimes students themselves
start clubs if there is an interest not represented.

Most of your friendships will emerge in these settings. You may spend
most of your time with the members of your immigrant rights group, a
cappella group, soccer team, or theater club. You are sharing high stress/high
gratification situations, getting to know each other in both good and hard
times. These experiences can forge bonds based on mutual respect for skills
you both value.

Sororities and fraternities have long traditions on many campuses and can also provide valuable ties spanning many generations. On the other hand, they can be hotbeds of pettiness and drunken mayhem. Those fraternities and sororities with traditions of service and high standards for behavior can be grounding. Where practices around selection processes involve cruelty, hazing, discrimination, or heavy drinking, however, you may want to think twice. These may be the "cool" groups on your campus, but do these practices represent who you are or how you want to be known?

The media presents far too many stories of tragedies resulting from what are supposed to be harmless and fun college pranks. Are you secure enough in your own values and goals that you can forgo being "in" to ensure that your activities are safe and purposeful? Your affiliations can make or break you. Choose them wisely.

A Story: Bill

Bill was one of the first Black students accepted to his Ivy League college in the 1960s. He was a solid student and became a campus leader. He was recruited by a fraternity that had been all white and had a national tradition of discrimination. Members of the local chapter, though, really accepted and valued Bill as a member. However, the national organization then forced the chapter out. As a result of this ugly situation, when Bill became president of the student body in his senior year, he worked to ban all fraternities from that campus. He knew from personal experience the harm that could result from racist behavior, and he worked the rest of his life to change those practices.

Info: Hazing

Hazing is defined as forcing a new or potential recruit (to the military, a college fraternity, etc.) to perform strenuous, humiliating, or dangerous tasks. Drinking to excess is a common hazing practice, as is engaging in acts that are totally degrading. Very often it goes too far. Google the Clearinghouse on Hazing Deaths. The site contains many cautionary tales, enough to justify the existence of an entire clearinghouse—a sobering thought, indeed.

DATING

Dating is a hugely important part of your college experience. You may even meet the love of your life. Dating is also a huge distraction (that is true in or out of college).

Much of what has been said about healthy friendships applies to dating as well. A good relationship is based on respect and friendship first. On the other hand, the reality is that "hooking up," or casual sex, is as likely to occur in college as anything more meaningful. In that case, being responsible is the issue. For both men and women, it means being sure to carry protection with you all the time. It also means avoiding situations where date rape is a potential outcome (for example, getting drunk at a frat party or somewhere where your drink can be spiked with a "date rape" drug).

Many campuses feature talks about safe behavior, but there are also resources to help with the outcomes of unsafe behavior. These can include the health center, counselors, advisors, and RAs.

There are so many books and websites on dating that I'm not going to take up a lot of space on the topic here, but I want to make a few points.

The best dating situations on a campus are the ones wherein you mutually nourish each other's successes. That may mean study dates, proofreading (not writing!) each other's papers, celebrating the A on a tough final, or insisting on actual sleep in the middle of finals instead of partying. The point is to take the long view and see that your partner achieves his or her goals, including finishing school.

Because so much of college life feels so intense and fraught with the pressure to get it right in that moment, dating can take on that pressure too. Increasingly, it is rare to find your soul mate during your college years. You may have a sense of the kind of person you want in your life, but you're still very much a work in progress, and so are those whom you're likely to date. (Sometimes great chemistry can overcome good sense.) You do not really solidify your sense of self until you're out in the work world and living on your own. So it is not the end of the world if a college relationship does not go the way you might hope. Both parties are figuring out a lot at the same time and in the same intense environment.

Just be sure to talk to someone—a parent, a friend, a therapist, a clergy-person—if you're feeling unhinged by an intimate relationship. Get it in perspective. We are amazingly resilient creatures. That said, it will be hard to remember this advice when the situation hits, but try your best to take this to heart so it does come to mind at that time.

A Story: Jose

Jose was a popular and attractive young man. He was a natural leader and would light up a room. As he began to grow and change at college he met Angela, who was ambitious, fun, smart, and beautiful. They became a couple, but Jose was also starting to realize that he had a deep passion for his religious faith.

In the midst of his junior year, he told his campus mentor that he had decided to enter the priesthood after graduation and would be applying to seminaries. His challenge was to explain this to Angela, who had begun to envision her life, and having children, with Jose. Her competition was not another woman, but the Catholic Church!

After discussing it with many friends, Jose was able to tell Angela with grace. Despite the difficult situation, they have remained good friends.

He is a now a priest and she an attorney. They have grown on very different paths, but value what they learned from their college relationship.

CLUBS AND ORGANIZATIONS

While you're building a great GPA and learning all sorts of new things in your classes, you should also be building toward your future by participating in clubs and extracurricular activities. This is where you learn or enhance your skills as a leader, team player, organizer, communicator, or artist. Clubs and activities are also where you're likely to make many of your friends, build your network, and expand your team.

These activities are also where you actually build a key part of your résumé. It's important, of course, for you to have internships, summer jobs or experiences, or work-study jobs, but these still cast you in the light of student or apprentice. When you serve as president of the debate team, director of the play, president of the class, editor of the paper, on a faculty search committee, as a peer advisor, or captain of the soccer team, you are manifesting your leadership abilities and people skills. When you're a member of a noteworthy club that does good work, that is to your credit too. These activities are affirmations of your abilities—to motivate and move others, to organize activities, and even to balance your own time well. They may be the source of conversation and shared interests at an interview. They can build your networks and relationships around passions you have in common with others.

Don't focus your extracurriculars solely on things related to your major, though. Your grades reveal only one aspect of who you are, just as a job is only part of your life. Each of us is multifaceted, and we need to use all the muscles we have. At my church I have a rule that I won't do on Sunday the same kinds of things I do at work during the week. I want to use other talents, such as my love of cooking, as my way of being of service there. You cannot spend every waking hour in the lab or library. It's good to get out and run or sing or dance or debate. Sometimes during these sorts of activities you actually do your best thinking. For example, I am often most creative, relative to work, when I'm baking.

While involvement in a club is excellent service in your college community, you may also want to think of service beyond the campus. Many say that college students were the winners in the 2008 presidential election. Students volunteered in record numbers to canvass, stuff envelopes, and do all manner of crucial work for the campaigns. But there are still many things you can do to serve the world now. Millions of young students need mentors, coaches, and tutors. There are cleanups to be undertaken and soup kitchens to be staffed. There is money to be raised. Advocacy and civic engagement are some of the most meaningful activities you can take on while you have the time during your school years. Students have often told me that the work they did as tutors, EMTs, or mentors has been the most gratifying and life-changing of their college careers.

Some campuses have volunteer offices or websites. Others have **service learning classes**, which build in the service as part of the course curriculum. Some colleges plan alternative spring breaks during which, instead of getting drunk in Fort Lauderdale, you build houses with Habitat for Humanity or clean out underbrush to prevent forest fires, or take your singing group on a tour of nursing homes. Trust me, you will come back from those trips feeling much better than your partying friends.

I would certainly opt to hire someone first who had a history of caring for others, so yes, extracurricular and service activities are résumé and network builders. But more important, they are character builders.

A Story: Seth

Seth was always active in community service in his high school and continued this work in college. His record of academic excellence and reputation as a leader through the debate team brought him to the attention of a dean, who recommended that he apply for the Rhodes and Marshall fellowships. Seth won the Marshall and was due to go to London in mid-September of 2001. Horrified by the September 11 attacks that had just occurred in the U.S., when he got to London he mobilized an effort to help college students at home learn more about our place in the world and how to address global challenges. He founded Americans for an Informed Democracy, which today promotes awareness and action to students on more than five thousand campuses around the world, providing solutions to issues on the campus, community, and national levels. See **www.aidemocracy.org** to learn what you can do on your campus.

EMPLOYERS

Many, if not most, of you will work while in college, so employers become part of your life too. The best jobs are the ones on campus—usually identified as **work-study**, part of your financial aid package. They do not involve back-and-forth travel and so save you time. And they have other benefits, such as helping you build your "team" of people. That is, they give you contacts within the administration and faculty and show you more about how your campus works. After all, it can only help to work in a dean's office or the president's office when you need recommendations! Another benefit of work-study jobs is the likelihood that there'll be an understanding ear when you ask to leave early or shift your hours to accommodate exams or papers.

Another excellent kind of job is one that relates to your major or potential career, building your résumé and contacts. If you're premed, you can find paid internships or part-time work in a hospital or nursing home. You can work in a city agency if you're a political science or urban affairs major, or at an embassy if you're a language major. In some cases, notably communications and journalism, internships are not paid, but the contacts you make are worth gold. Prestigious internship programs supported by industry, such as

INROADS (**www.INROADS.org**), SIFE (Students in Free Enterprise), and others are also competitive but rewarding. Some schools have funds to help students on scholarship be able to afford to take unpaid internships. Check with your campus financial aid office and career services/internship office.

Finally there are the unglamorous jobs that pay the bills. They can range from working at a restaurant to paralegal positions. Use your college career office to find the best of these. Even these "pay jobs," though, have value beyond a paycheck. Their common denominator is what they can show about you. If you maintain your GPA, lead or join a club, and hold a job, you clearly know something about managing time and setting priorities. The employment section of a résumé can show ever-increasing levels of responsibility, continuity, and value added. Your employer can become a reference for you later. So it is important to be on time, be courteous to all at your workplace, and be willing to jump in and be helpful, learn new skills, and show initiative. Your dress, your attitude, and your demeanor all count in this context. Keeping your job may also keep you in college if it helps to pay the bills.

On the other hand, you are not the first priority of your employers. They do not have patience for your being late, using your cell phone, or researching a paper during working hours. They have brought you in to do a job and perhaps learn a craft. You need to play by their rules, even if you do not always agree or have great chemistry with the boss or your coworkers. This is, as they say, the real world. The winners will be those who demonstrate the most maturity by being gracious when they don't feel like it, dressing the part when jeans would be much more comfortable, or offering to help a colleague with a project even though it is not their responsibility to do so. Rolling your eyes, wearing skimpy tank tops, and saying something is not your job will not get you the references or opportunities you want. And being pleasant does count.

A Story: Elena

Elena could not afford college without a job. She thought she wanted to be a lawyer and so, the summer before she started college, she took a job as an assistant at a small law firm. As she progressed through school she also progressed at the firm. Eventually, though she was not there full-time, she was promoted to office manager and oversaw all the functions that kept the firm moving smoothly. The firm's partners became her mentors, teaching her about the law, and they wrote some of her recommendations for law school. Elena managed to also stay involved with one club at school, and through it became visible to the college administration, which helped her successfully navigate through the law school application process. She now heads her own small firm practicing family law on Wall Street. In the end, Elena learned all she needed to know about running her practice through the job she took to pay for college.

DEANS AND OTHER ADMINISTRATORS

Having been a dean in several schools, I'm often asked what on earth deans do. Our main job is to help students graduate.

We advise, we troubleshoot the most challenging problems, and we help establish the processes, programs, and procedures that make college work. We often have individuals and departments working for us, but not always.

Ideally, deans are caring people—they are among your "people." My niece was rushed to a hospital from her college dormitory, and the dean at her school called her mother and sat at the bedside for twenty-four hours. In my own time as a dean, I have dealt with conflicts with professors and guided students to jobs, fellowships, and counseling services. I have delivered homework to the infirmary. I have dealt with cases of plagiarism, drunkenness, late papers, depression, and divorces.

The deans can be your best allies. Do not fear them. In the case of late papers, if you can make a good case, deans can help get **extensions** or deal with other exceptions to policy. You have to be honest with them, however, and ideally, approach them before a crisis occurs. Deans may also contact you. They'll tell you if you're behind on requirements, or if, for instance, you should apply for the Goldwater Fellowship, or if a professor has complained that you are continuously late. Good or bad, it is not a good idea to ignore messages from a dean's office, as they usually signal something you need to know about or pay attention to.

Info: College Administration

Colleges are like any other big organizations—they have their own hierarchy (and perhaps bureaucracy!).

- They are governed at the very top by a president, who reports to a Board of Trustees (prominent figures, possibly including alumni, businesspersons, educators, and influential individuals with ties to the government, organizations, and other individuals with financial resources). The board has an obligation to see that the institution is well managed.

- Below and reporting to the president will be an Office of the Provost, who is typically the chief academic officer, overseeing the faculty and curricular issues. (This may vary from campus to campus.)

- There may be a Dean of the Faculty (who oversees the policies and issues relating to faculty), a Chief Financial or Chief Administrative Officer (this officer keeps the money flowing and the lights on), and a Dean or Vice President for Student Affairs. The vice president for student affairs has a large portfolio, which can include enrollment services (admissions, financial aid, bursar, and registrar); athletics; physical and mental health services; residential life; religious affairs; student activities and clubs; and more. When I held that office, for example, I also had responsibility for marketing as it related to admissions.

- There are usually deans for each academic unit or college, such as the Dean of Arts and Sciences or the Dean of Engineering, and for each graduate or professional school, such as the Dean of the Graduate School of Arts and Sciences, the Dean of the School of Medicine, or the Dean of the School of Law. These deans may report to the provost or the president, and are responsible for the academic guidance of their school.
- **Academic advisors, Counseling Services, Residential Hall Advisors, or other advising services** may be housed in the portfolio of either an academic dean or the dean or vice president for student affairs.

You should seek help from the administration when needed—indeed, it is your right to do so. But it's important to know who to go to, so you do not waste time or step on toes.

If there is a faculty member, advisor, or administrator that you are comfortable with already, you may take your issue to that person to discuss and develop the right strategy for dealing with your concern. Sometimes upperclassmen can guide you to the right person or to someone who's been helpful to them.

For academic concerns relating to faculty or departmental issues, the place to begin is usually the department chair. If you don't get satisfaction there, move up to the dean to whom the chairs report.

Do not go directly to the president with your problem, as the issue will just be sent back down to the appropriate person and resolution will be delayed. To find the right person, the college website usually has a section on administration that reveals the particular organization of your school. Do not go directly to the president with your problem, as the issue will just be sent back down to the appropriate person and resolution will be delayed. Another way to get to know your way around the college administration is to be part of the student government or serve on committees that enable you to interact with those who govern.

Another crucial office to be aware of is the **Career Services** office. The Career Services office exists to assist you with processes such as writing résumés or finding internships or jobs. It has long job listings from employers eager to hire students while they are in college or right after. These positions can range from internships to entry level to substantive career-track jobs, typically geared for alumni. The office may have lists from major national firms and also from smaller or more local firms and organizations. It is in the college's interest to be sure that its students represent it well, so the office works with you to be sure your résumé is as polished as your shoes and your social and interviewing skills are beyond reproach.

Many free workshops and panel discussions are offered, where experts and alumni may share with you their wisdom and experience to help you make good career choices and successfully navigate the path to a job. As you prepare for interviews, you can do necessary research on the firms and industries you are targeting by using the office's libraries and other resources. And the office may offer mock interviews. Watch for career weeks or career fairs, and note whether you have to register with the office to get the alerts. The websites are a treasure trove of information.

If you purchased the career office's services on the open market after you graduate, they would cost thousands of dollars. You get them free—which is to say you paid for them with your tuition—so use them. The mistake many students make is waiting until second semester of the senior year to tap this resource. That is too late. Start no later than your second year to start using career services and to seek internships.

A Story: Nouhoum

Nouhoum was a hardworking student born in Mali, West Africa. He had an outstanding academic record, but no meaningful jobs, community service, or activities on his résumé. The dean, who noted his 3.9 GPA in economics, contacted him to find out his plans. When she saw his résumé, she took him to the career services office, which helped him find an internship at a major bank. He also began to take part in a club and to work with a mentor. By the time he graduated, the bank where he had interned offered him a job. He also got an offer for a position at the UN, which he accepted. Because of his work experience and his service to others, Nouhoum then secured a job aimed at poverty alleviation and was able to move back to his own country to do work.

If you find yourself lucky or smart enough to participate in a special program on your campus, another great resource will be the director or advisor of that program. Especially in large schools, these programs may be a way to be part of a smaller community within the larger school. Some are enrichment programs with an academic focus, such as the McNair program mentioned earlier. Others have an ethnic or gender focus, such as Philander Smith College's Black Male Initiative. Some may be career focused, such as the international SIFE (Students in Free Enterprise), also mentioned earlier. The faculty or administrators who oversee these programs offer wonderful guidance and personalized attention to participating students. They are often the ones who can pinpoint students who should aspire further or help those who are faltering.

Tutors in **study centers** are also part of your support team—you can get everything from math tutoring to aid in writing papers. While professors or TAs will give assistance with particular courses, a tutoring center offers generalized help, such as with study skills. For example, the way you study biology, which is heavy on memorization, is different from the way you study English literature, where you are dealing with a more interpretive framework. They also offer help particular to certain disciplines. For example, a language lab is the place for help with both speaking and reading a foreign language.

The reality, though, is that these various centers are used most often by the best students who want to move from a B+ to an A, while too often those students who are struggling at the C or D level are more likely to crawl under the covers. While some students think that using these resources marks them as dumb, the truth is that smart individuals know what they don't know and get help from those who do know. Plus, you pay for these study centers through your tuition dollars, and they are free.

Learning centers or other resources also exist for those students who may learn differently or have a physical disability. Having **learning disabilities** that have been verified by testing makes students eligible for special services and support that can include extra time on exams or permission to type rather than handwrite in-class exercises. Students with physical disabilities, such as deafness or blindness, are entitled, through the **Americans with Disabilities Act (ADA)**, to special services and support as well. Campuses must provide physically disabled students with physical access to buildings as well as resources such as signing or special computers. A specific office usually helps students with these or any other special needs.

Finally, do not forget the libraries and **librarians**. It may seem to you that libraries, those massive structures filled with books, are old-fashioned, but they are actually overflowing with resources. In addition to the books are many online resources, including a huge variety of publications, such as **academic journals** (periodicals where scholars publish articles about their subject areas and research) and magazines, newspapers, and other materials from all over the world. They can be very useful in job-related research as well as looking for scholarships, in addition to the research you do for classes. You can also find the books, articles, films, and other material that your professors put **on reserve** for students to access at no cost. Some campuses provide laptops on loan while you're in the library.

Whether you're doing research for a course, a job, or a scholarship, the librarians can turn out to be your best friends. They are highly trained in information technology and can guide you to exactly the sources and materials you need (they also help you learn to do this on your own). They are a gold mine.

Libraries are also quiet places to study. Sometimes they contain study rooms, or **carrels**, where you can leave your materials (not your laptop!) when you are deep into a project. During exams you may even be able to spend the night there!

Info: Email Etiquette

The email below was sent out by an advisor to her premed students as an example of how not to communicate with administrators or others whose support you need. Secretaries, advisors, and others can make or break your future career.

This is an actual email that was received by another prehealth advisor at another college. Needless to say, all the other advisors thought this person extremely ignorant about professional demeanor and communication, and we laughed at the student who wrote this! I wanted to share in case any of you thought that the message below seemed okay!

Shorthand is fine for emails and texts to friends. It is completely unacceptable when you send a message to someone in authority or someone you do not know. It is the same regarding the use of someone's first name when you have not asked permission to use it! Just thought this was important enough to share.

> "HI ITS ME BIMBO,I CAME TO YOUR OFFICE ON FRIDAY BUT I WAS TOLD YOU LL NT BE ON SIT UNTIL MONDAY,HAVE NOT BEEN FEELIN FINE FOR SOME DAYS NOW,I DONT KNOW IF I COULD WRITE MY TEST ANOTHER DAY.I WILL BE WAITING FOR YOUR REPLY MA."

Later we look at other persons and offices that are there for you when you hit a wall—colleges give you a long list that starts to look as if you have a Verizon-size team backing you up.

Some of your people resources are used differently at different points in your academic life. You may rely more heavily on some, like advisors or even the librarian, in your first year as you find your way around. Whereas the career office will become of ever-increasing importance as you get closer and closer to graduation. It is important to know how the sequence of experiences takes place every year so you also know how "your people" will fit in.

Chapter 7
TRANSITIONS

College can be like a dress rehearsal for the rest of your life. You are becoming more self-sufficient, learning how to manage your own time, finding your own voice as a writer, paying your own way and budgeting, traveling far from home, getting help when you need it, managing relationships with persons of backgrounds very different from yours—the list goes on. These skills are the same ones you apply as an employee, graduate student, or mature and successful adult. At each phase of college, you are expected to engage these skills more and more fully.

Each year of college builds on the one before. Though it may not be apparent, there is logic to the progression. Whether you're a beginning student of traditional age (around eighteen) in a traditional campus setting or an older returning student with a full array of responsibilities on an urban campus, the logic prevails, with some variations. It is best not to rush through or try to skip parts of the experience, because you will miss something important. Let's look at each year's purpose and its prominent facets.

A Story: Josefina

As a sophomore, Josefina became interested in the research that one of her professors was doing on children's learning styles. She contacted the professor, who invited Josefina to work with her. By her junior year Josefina was invited to join the NIMH/COR program (National Institutes of Mental Health–Career Opportunities in Research Program), which funded her continued research and her professor's mentoring. That year she was able to attend a conference in the Midwest. There she met faculty from two other schools doing similar work. She had never considered leaving her native urban area, but really liked the researchers and scholars she met. The graduate schools actively tried to recruit her and flew her in to visit during the summer before her senior year. Josefina later landed in a doctoral program at one of the schools. This would not have happened had she not attended the conference and presented the work she had done with her professor.

FIRST YEAR

There is no question that the first semester of the first year is the most critical. Many studies show that this is the time when students are most likely to drop out of college, if not permanently, then temporarily. It is when many consider transferring (though most don't). There are various factors that go into this.

Remember that college is meant to be a transitional point for you from being the responsibility of others to being responsible for yourself. Before, parents, teachers, and coaches always told you what to do and when to do it. In college, while there are rules, suddenly you are expected to figure things out for yourself. No one makes you do your homework. Assignments are rarely daily, and it's unusual to be quizzed on the previous night's reading. You're obliged to find help if you need it. Most often there are no curfews or bed checks. No more babysitters!

So, one of three things happens. You may breathe a sigh of relief and take charge of your life in a mature way, getting rest when you need it, making friends who are good for you, getting assignments done on time, partying in moderation. Or you go crazy with the freedom, partying every night, making friends with persons who would petrify your parents, putting off assignments until the night before they're due. Or you become overwhelmed by the many options. I have seen all three scenarios, in the extreme and in moderation.

I have also seen many students become intimidated by their classmates. I had that kind of experience when I got to college. In high school, like many of you, I was in lots of clubs and activities. In particular, I edited the high school yearbook. I thought that made me pretty special. But it seemed that everyone in my freshman class was a yearbook editor. Suddenly I was not so special or so smart.

Just remember, you were all accepted to your school because you met certain standards within a reasonable range. Each of you brings different skills and experiences. All of you are insecure.

But some act with bravado, as if they know it all. For instance, a student whose parent attended the same school may show off his insider status based on his parent's experience. But that student brings his own strengths and weaknesses and still has to navigate whatever changes have taken place in the twenty-plus years since the parent was there. That student also carries the burden of higher parental and perhaps institutional expectations. For all the bravado, he is scared too.

Perhaps the majority of students just become quiet, figuring that if you don't ask questions, no one knows how much you don't know. This doesn't work, because you won't find the answers if you don't ask the questions—and there are so many in this new environment. Too many students sit in class or participate in other activities, collectively clueless and likely to remain so, because no one has the guts to 'fess up to needing to ask questions.

Others try to do everything at once. Because you were quite active in high school, partly to get into college, you may believe you have to do that again. Instead, you need to slow it down so you can learn your way around and focus your talents in the best places. You were among the best from your secondary school, and now you're just one of many. And that is all right. Colleges want you to become the best of who you are now.

You may be returning to school after creating a work life or working and starting a family, so you may be older than most of your classmates. That may feel uncomfortable. You may be closer in age to your faculty and feel that you've lost time, or you may have lost a job and need to build a new set of skills. You are not alone. My experience, and that of other administrators, is that you may be a better focused and determined student. You are motivated to do what's necessary, and you have less time to play, so you use your time wisely and well. Remember the story of Pauli Murray, who returned to school four times to create four different careers for herself. You are never too old—I once had a graduate assistant who was fabulous and earning a second degree at the age of sixty-eight.

Personal Challenges

Among the new experiences you'll have in your first year is separation from the familiar. You have to make new friends, learn new spaces, live or hang out with different people, perhaps eat unfamiliar foods, learn new ways of learning, and be guided by new rules. That is a lot of *new* at one time. It helps at first, if you're on a residential campus, to bring some of your favorite things with you—a stuffed animal, music, a favorite bedspread or poster, photos. And today, technology makes staying connected to the familiar a lot easier via email or Facebook. At first it's tempting to stay closely connected to your old friends. A huge lift for me my first semester was a dozen birthday roses sent by a high school best friend. But especially if your friends are at different campuses or living different kinds of lives, then you may have less and less to talk about. So, you should begin to make new friends. One or two is just fine to start. She may be a roommate. He may be someone you meet at orientation. You need to have someone to talk, eat, and see a movie with. Your circle will expand over time as you get more involved in your courses and extracurricular activities.

You may be encountering a far more diverse population in ethnicity, nationality, religion, gender, and economic status than you have known before—many high schools are fairly homogeneous, as are the communities they serve. On many if not most campuses, some official is responsible for dealing with diversity issues. Offices offer chaplains, rabbis, or other religious leaders. Clubs and programs may serve your particular ethnic group, nationality, or faith.

If your sexual orientation is not heterosexual, you can also find friendly campuses. Some actively recruit gay students, and many others try to ensure that all students are safe and feel at ease. The site **www.campuspride.org** may be helpful.

These programs and groups that target ethnic, national, racial, religious, sexual, and other identities can be a great comfort, and you should not shy from engaging with them if they help you ease into campus life more smoothly. They are not stigmatizing and, in fact, may allow you to celebrate your identity with pride and solidarity and share it with the larger campus community. They are a source of strength that should empower you to move into the mainstream of campus life with greater self-awareness and more security about your identity. Such groups are also a great way to make friends whose experiences may more closely mirror your own.

Settling In

In the first year, you will have **orientations** of various sorts—they are of the utmost importance. They may range from a day to a week and may be on or off campus. In some cases you can register for classes on a priority basis during orientation. Time may be set aside to get to know your new classmates in fun and casual ways. A vast amount of information is presented, usually along with a handbook or website tips. You won't remember everything you hear, so it's wise to identify someone whom you feel you might go to when you need to talk. The person could be your advisor or your RA, an upperclassman, a peer advisor, a dean, or a chaplain.

This year you are taking the fundamental courses on which all your other learning will build. The required writing course may seem bothersome, especially if you consider yourself a good writer, but it teaches you to write differently. In high school you fed back what the teacher gave you. In college, you are expected to find your own voice, put forth your own theories, and back up your thinking with solid evidence. The first year may be the only time professors help with grammar and structure. After that it is likely assumed that you've learned those skills. Plagiarism is discussed during the first year. If you fall afoul of those rules, officials may cut you some slack, but not after that.

The math or biology principles you need to understand are taught in first-year courses. If you don't get them then, you'll struggle greatly later on in related classes that may be part of your major, such as chemistry or economics. This is the time to be sure you're placed on the right class level, that you're seeking tutoring or support, and that you're sharing with an advisor any struggles you're having with these entry-level courses. Every student arrives with different levels of preparation, skill, and aptitude in various subjects. You are not the only one who may be seeking help. We'll say it again: it is essential to seek help if you need it.

A **first-year experience course** of some sort may also be offered, which is designed to ensure that you understand how college works both academically and in terms of key resources, such as library use. The course may also be an introduction to crucial learning skills, ranging from writing to gathering evidence, which will dominate your college experience.

You may find yourself registered in what are called **blocks**, in which you're grouped with other students for core courses, but split for electives. These blocks may be organized by career area or potential-major interest that you may have indicated in your application. Your group could be all premed or all business students taking the introductory courses for that field. This method allows you to connect with your classmates and form study groups or friendships more easily.

Increasingly, schools including Purdue University and the University of Cincinnati offer the option of being in a **learning community**, which can be residential (when students are grouped in a particular residence hall), or nonresidential (when students just attend classes together). These programs cluster students and faculty around common themes, texts, or even backgrounds. They allow for getting better acquainted with classmates and professors, providing more opportunities to share ideas and integrate learning and life. Florida Memorial is among some other schools offering a freshman studies program, which groups first-year courses and coordinates the resource needs of new students. Specialized programs even exist for premed students, such as the American Medical Association's Virtual Mentor Program, which is Web-based and allows students to connect with mentors.

Many colleges check on first-year students at midterm, and if professors report heavy absences or poor grades on early tests or papers, then you are likely to get a note from your advisor or dean. If you get such a note, *please* pay attention! These are early warning signs. Unless you deal with such issues now, your situation is not likely to get better by itself. But it can get better.

A Cautionary Tale:
Murray Ignores the Warnings

Murray was a smart kid from a good high school. He got into the college of his choice and once there discovered that, in contrast to his high school experience, he was quite popular. Away from the eyes of his parents overseeing his homework or his class attendance, he spent a lot more time partying than going to his college classes and studying. He ignored the messages from the dean and his instructors, and he began to fail his courses. He also kept these failures from his parents. Because of the Buckley amendment, which protects student privacy, they did not know how much trouble he was in until the college asked him to take a year off. Then his parents learned that Murray had been given many warnings and had ignored them all until it was too late. Despite his pleadings that he would do better, he had to spend the year at home, where he took courses, held a job, and learned much about himself. He returned to college to complete his degree, but he was now a year behind his class.

Lesson learned: As soon as you are issued a warning or see a pattern of poor grades emerging, get help!

In your first year in college, you are taking your first steps toward establishing mature responsibility for yourself in a safe space. The consequences of making a hash of it now are far less risky than if you were in a job or other major responsibility. That is not to say that you can get away with serious offenses (violence, an F average, serious substance abuse), which do and should have appropriately severe consequences. But there is more forgiveness in the first year than you will ever have later in life. And there is more support for getting it right than you will ever have in the later years.

Info: Books and Materials

This may sound silly, but sometimes students try to get through courses without the assigned books—I have seen it happen. Do not do this! Books may be expensive, but they are where the information is. Ideally your instructors will not simply recite in class what you are expected to read. More likely they will comment on and discuss the assigned material. They will ask questions that assume you have done the reading, and if class participation is required, then you will be in trouble if you don't have a clue about what is being discussed. The midterm or final exam will likely include references to the lecture or seminar discussion *and* to the readings.

Assigned readings can come in various forms. The syllabus will tell you what to expect. Some readings may be books you will have to buy, or they may be **on reserve** in the library. Some will be articles you can find on the Web, on reserve, or in a **course pack** prepared by the instructor specifically for the course—these can usually be bought at the campus or local bookstore or at the local copy center near or affiliated with your campus. If your professor uses **Blackboard** or another course networking site, some materials may be posted there. Course packs contain shorter items (such as a book chapter) so that you don't have to pay for the entire book. (Some royalties go to authors for this type of usage; copying whole chapters without permission would cheat them out of getting paid for use of their material.) The instructor will specify the edition of a particular book. You need to pay attention to this, as pages assigned will align with that edition and probably not with earlier, outdated ones. New editions may also contain new information you will need, especially in the sciences or technology.

If the same edition is used every year for your course, however, you can save money in a variety of ways. Buy the paperback instead of the hardcover if you can. Compare prices between your campus bookstore and online book sites. If you can find a used copy of the edition, you can get discounts sometimes as high as 90 percent off the full price.

A sufficient number of copies for each course will have been ordered for the campus bookstore, but increasingly there are online resources for books, even beyond Amazon. Some websites even customize texts according to faculty needs, such as those offered on **http://flatworldknowledge.com**, where you can download some texts for free. There is a new resource at **http://www.chegg.com**, which lets you rent your textbooks (which means you can't mark them up). If you want to keep them at term's end, you pay full price, so this route can be costly. The Kindle® (from Amazon), an e-book reader, simulates a book-type format and can hold thousands of volumes; it offers many fiction titles. Apple's iPad can also function as a book reader. An e-reader may be pricey, but it is convenient if you are commuting and have to carry heavy loads of books.

You can buy used books from the campus store or books being sold by other students. (But don't buy a book that is all marked up, as you may want to highlight different passages than the previous owner did.) You can also sell many of your course books back to the bookstore or to other students, but you may want or need to use some books over and over, such as a basic economics text if that is your major, or a great novel. My children actually used some of my old college texts when they were undergrads.

There are several reasons to own books or materials, rather than counting on reserve copies, rentals, or Kindle. The downside of some of these lower-cost strategies is that you can't mark up books for future reference—you have to take extensive notes as you read. Other students may be using the one or two reserve copies at your school library when you go to look for a text. When you own a book, you have the flexibility of studying when and where you want to—you can read on the subway or bus or in your jammies at 3 a.m. And perhaps you will fall in love with a book and want to keep it forever. You may need to refer back to a volume for future courses or even find it relevant to your life experiences.

The bottom line is that you can't *not* read what is assigned. That leads only to failure!

Changing Your Mind

The first year is the point of greatest attrition from college. It can happen that at some point in the first year you begin to realize you're in over your head, you're really uncomfortable being away from home, or the culture is too different. This is not at all uncommon in the first semester, and many students claim by Thanksgiving that they want to transfer or leave school. By the second semester, students typically find their footing and continue right where they are.

For some, however, that gut feeling does not go away. Others have made some bad decisions that have led to academic tragedy. Perhaps a failing grade has resulted from not asking questions or too much social life. Your GPA falls below the acceptable level, and the school asks you to take a leave of absence. Then you decide either that college is not right for you at all or that this college is not the right one.

You decide to either **drop out** or **transfer**. Dropping out is never a good idea. If you are asked to take a leave, keep taking courses somewhere and develop a plan to return as soon as you are allowed and your situation permits. You may need to regroup financially if you have lost a scholarship. But plan to return. Remember that your earning ability for the rest of your life depends on this degree.

You may be right, however, that you'll be better off in a different environment. Perhaps you chose a big school and realize that a smaller one is better for you. Or you discovered a new field and another school has more resources devoted to it. You may want a more faith-based environment or an urban setting instead of a rural one. In these cases, transferring is worth exploring, rather than not attending college at all.

Before beginning the process of transferring, talk to advisors at your current school to see if there may be other ways to address the issues making you feel uncomfortable. Often there are. It is likely in any event that you'll need some sort of signoff from your current campus for your application to the new one, and that may be the trigger for the conversation about your concerns.

If you've done well where you are now, you may be able to transfer easily to a different school. In some cases, transfer is nearly automatic, as when you move from a two-year to a four-year school in a public system. It is harder if you have not done well. In that case, the strategy of taking a leave of absence and courses elsewhere may be the right one—whether you return to your old school or find another that fits better.

In any event, you must find out which credits transfer to the new school. Do not expect that they all will—this is one good reason to not transfer. You will basically have to start again under a new set of requirements. Likely you will lose money on courses you took and paid for that the new school won't count. For this reason, it's best to transfer earlier in your academic career rather than later—you have less to lose. Think hard about transferring before you take the action.

There are many things you will discover in your first year. One, which you may not expect, is that sometimes sophomore students can look smug. This is not because they are arrogant, but because they are proud they have survived the first year. You'll make it too.

SOPHOMORE YEAR

Though first-year students often think second years have it all figured out, sophomores have their own set of challenges. There is often talk of a "sophomore slump," a feeling of coming down after a period of exhilaration. Initially, once the excitement of the new has worn off, temporary boredom can set in—sometimes it can even look like depression.

In your freshman year, you are elated with new experiences and your family's pride that you made it to college. By second year you know your way around the campus, have made some friends, have an idea of your strengths and weaknesses, and perhaps have reached some decisions about your future. Attention is on the new group of first years coming in, and you may even be asked to help welcome and orient them.

Whereas during your first year, the school thrust resources at you, by your second year, you are expected to know what and where they are and to access them yourself. You are now considered more mature and expected to stand on your own feet. Now you are expected to take advantage of all the available tools and resources to keep moving forward.

You have now taken most of your introductory and/or required courses and can move up to the next level of rigor. You have more room in your schedule for elective classes—these are important. Some fill certain requirements, but also they give you a chance to explore your future major. Sophomore year should be a time of exploration. Take classes in subjects you have never heard of, such as anthropology, or in areas you don't know much about but think might be interesting, such as art history. You may find new pathways, new strengths, new interests, and perhaps new career ideas.

The sophomores you met as freshmen are now juniors, engaged in their major departments. They are now sources of information about what it's like to be in those departments and which courses they like. Don't forget, this is one of the last chances you'll have for intellectual play.

Looking Ahead

This is the year you **declare your major**. Typically, when you have about sixty credits (the end of the second year), you are mandated by your school, or sometimes your funding sources at the local level, to declare what you intend to major or concentrate in. At that point you have reviewed the catalog or the website for all the requirements of the major and have met the prerequisites to enter that major. You should have met with the major's designated advisor. It's also a good idea to meet with seniors in the major to learn what their experiences have been. You may want to learn what alumni for your region are doing now.

The particular process that formalizes the major declaration varies from school to school, but in order for the major to be listed on your transcript, the declaration must get to the registrar. You may also want to add a minor if your school provides this option. You have to make sure though that all the pieces fit in terms of the number and nature of courses you need to fulfill a major and a minor (and any other requirements, such as a foreign language). You may want to be cautious about the burden of a minor, which can look good on a résumé, but has more requirements to manage. If you have a passion for a subject area besides your major, you can always take the courses as electives. In some cases, they may fit well with your major and even fulfill some major requirements. You could find, at some point, that you have enough credits in the subject for it to become a minor with little difficulty. In many cases, though, it's better to take the classes for enjoyment and to claim a concentration on your résumé. For now, take advantage of both your advising center and the advisor in your major while you make these plans.

If you're on a premed track, the beginning of the year is a good time to meet with the advisor who works with students considering **medical school**. In your freshman year you should have taken at least biology and perhaps chemistry. By your second year, based on how you did in those courses and how well you enjoyed them, you know if this is the direction for you. Often students think they want to be doctors because they want to help humanity, or they've been inspired by the care given a sick loved one, or their parents want it. But there is more to the field and preparation for it than those motivations may support. You do need to be good at science and math, even though you do not have to major in those areas. You do have to take two terms of biology and chemistry, and one each of organic chemistry, calculus, and physics. And you must do well in those courses. They are the foundations for your MCAT tests later.

If you found in your freshman year that you hated these courses, or that they were a struggle, and they began to affect your GPA negatively, then the **premed advisor** can give you a reality check before you go farther; he or she can offer options that may better suit you. On the other hand, if you did really well in these classes and loved them, then you have two choices. You can look at careers in medicine, or you can consider scientific research in a college, industry, or government. Fields that do not require a medical degree, but which are lucrative, range from physician's assistant to anesthesiologist's assistant. The premed advisor can explain your options, as well as the necessary next steps, including information about different types of programs and the pros and cons of medical schools abroad. To prepare for next year, you might consider the option of applying during your sophomore year for science fellowships you would use as a junior. Or you might join a premed club or society on your campus.

Those considering careers in nursing or physical therapy also need to be sure they're on track in terms of courses. If you do have an interest and aptitude in medical-related fields, demand is great and growing. The number of students applying to medical schools has declined, and for those who want to serve rural or low-income populations, funding to help defray some of the costs may even be available.

Branching Out

Although we cautioned you about overloading on too many clubs and activities in your first year, now may be a good time to take on more and even emerge into leadership roles. By now you know what is available and more about what you like to do and are best at. These activities begin to build up the experience that can make your résumé stand out. Although your career path may not be clear to you, it is beneficial to show early on that you can lead, you can manage your time, and you have passion for one or more causes or issues.

If there are resources on your campus that are directly related to service, civic engagement, or leadership development, then take advantage of them now. Bethune-Cookman College in Florida, for instance, has a Center for Civic Engagement.

An easy way to connect to this arena is to take courses labeled **service learning** or **community-based learning**. Increasing numbers of campuses offer such classes, which have a service component embedded within them, such as researching community resources for the mayor's office or hands-on work in a day-care center. Portland State University and Macalester College are two examples that make service experiences central to their institutional approach. You are integrating classroom learning with real-life applications of that knowledge. Such work is personally gratifying, while also being real-life, credit-bearing applications of that knowledge. It may even affect your career.

Many more students are now reporting interest in public service careers, and numerous options in the new economy are in health care, education, and the environment, which lend themselves well to undergraduate service internships or courses.

By your senior year, when you apply for graduate programs or jobs, you will have built a track record of at least two years of experience highlighting your capabilities. Newspaper interviews with Drew Faust about her background for the presidency of Harvard University noted her campus leadership as class president in her sophomore year at Bryn Mawr College. Some fellowships—including the Truman or Goldwater, which you apply for as a junior—look to your sophomore-year activities as indicators of your passions.

The sophomore year is also a good time to lock in what you have learned by helping to guide new students. Take advantage of chances to lead campus tours, to be a "big brother" or "sister" to a freshman, or to speak to groups of first years or applicants. When guiding others, you solidify your own knowledge and may learn some things along the way. This kind of exchange keeps you engaged and growing.

Info: Two-Year Schools

There is no question that some college experience is better than none in terms of skills, new knowledge, and ultimately, earning capacity. For many students, life circumstances, including finances, limit options to the two-year degree. Community colleges are designed to fast-track your experience and ensure that you gain as much as you can in the time available. You get to participate in clubs, research, service, and all the other experiences that come with college life.

Community colleges are one of the best deals around. They are less costly per year than most four-year colleges and are usually publicly subsidized. If you are in a community college or enrolled in an associate's degree program, you are finished in two years. In some ways, four years are compressed into two. You have to learn the ropes faster, engage immediately in any remediation or catching up you need to do, and decide *very* fast what your concentration or path will be. In some ways your sophomore year in a community college is also your senior year, and so all that here applies to seniors may well apply to you if you are graduating with an associate's degree.

Community colleges and associate's degree programs tend to be inherently vocational. You may want to stop school after getting that degree, once you have the professional credential that may come with it. Or you can look at the degree as your first, or the college as a place to retool. You can strengthen your skills or get comfortable being on a college campus. You may discover new skills and love of learning and use the two years to prepare to transfer to a four-year degree or institution, saving money along the way.

JUNIOR YEAR

Your third year can be daunting. You are past the halfway point of your college career, and every day now brings you closer to its end. By now you realize the extent to which college is like a cocoon, and a very comfortable one at that. What comes next seems amorphous. You also realize that there are more classes you want to take, but don't have the time, what with meeting your major requirements and other classes you have left. There is often a vague sense of pressure.

Advisement may become a different process. You declared your major at the end of the sophomore year (maybe before). Now your advisor is in your department and will guide you through the rules and requirements and also the opportunities of the major. You may need to touch bases now and then with the central advising office or the registrar to be sure all of your graduation requirements are being met. Most campuses now have websites, so you can track your own progress.

Sometimes departments hold meetings or events to introduce new students to the department and its guidelines. It is here that you get approval to take any off-campus courses that relate to the discipline or for any exceptions to departmental rules; you also register any concerns about faculty here.

The department bulletin boards may list relevant jobs, events, or internships that don't show up elsewhere on campus. Check them often. Flyers unique to the department are also often posted or distributed here.

The department chair—a very important person to know—manages the faculty and the curriculum and mediates any student issues. The other key person is the department administrator, who often has the power to sign off on key items and accept materials meant for faculty, and who can even track them down for you. Treat these administrators well—they may end up knowing you better than anyone else in the department. They often have longevity and know the quirks of a department's players and systems.

A Cautionary Tale: Jeff's Bad Behavior

Jeff was a good student set on a career in medicine. The premed advisor, along with her administrative assistant, was located in the dean's office. The assistant was responsible for maintaining student files and records and for seeing that the files were prepared for review by a faculty committee, which wrote recommendations for medical schools.

Jeff haunted the office daily, and in fact became a nuisance. The office served at least a hundred students, but he behaved as though he were the only one who counted. On occasion he was rude to the assistant (though obsequious to the advisor), and his actions frequently upset her.

The advisor heard about Jeff's behavior, which she brought to the attention of the faculty committee. The members agreed that such conduct would not reflect well on the college nor serve the profession well, and so the committee's recommendations were not as positive as they might otherwise have been.

> _Lessons learned:_ Treat everyone with respect, particularly those in a position to help and serve you. They may have more influence than you know.

Major Decisions

In your junior year you start to think about the future in a more serious way, for example venturing off-campus to study abroad or to begin internships or perhaps planning for graduate school.

If you plan to continue in school after college, now is the time to begin discussions with your faculty or a graduate advisor (both would be best) about graduate school. The reality is that by the end of junior year you are taking tests and lining up potential schools and developing personal statements. A **graduate school fair** may be held on your campus or nearby, or even at conferences you may attend. Be sure to go and collect information, but also contacts for your applications. Making a good impression with a professor or recruiter at a fair can lead to an interview. This is similar to a job fair, so approach it with the same professionalism and preparation.

Your professors in your major can tell you about their personal knowledge of schools, programs, and faculty in your area of interest. If opportunities to do research with a professor come up, either through a grant or program, grab the chance. It could even lead to presenting your work at an academic conference or attending one with your professor, where you can meet faculty—and sometimes recruiters—from graduate programs you may consider later. Making a good impression can open up options at schools you didn't believe were possibilities.

You will also plan to take GRE, MCAT, LSAT, or GMAT graduate tests at the end of the year or during the summer between junior and senior years. The fall is _not_ too early to begin to take test prep courses (look for those offered or subsidized by your school, as well as at Kaplan and Princeton Review, which can offer scholarships or discounts). Students often make the mistake of assuming that they can prepare, by themselves, a month before these exams. Those who do well on these crucial career tests begin to pace their study months ahead. If you have not been a good test taker, don't limit your career choices by test avoidance. Use every tool you can to prepare for the test—you may need it for the graduate study appropriate for your goals.

Reading is one of the most valuable preparation activities you can do to prepare for the test. A stumbling block for many students on these tests is not the content, but comprehension of the questions, the vocabulary, and the use of language. This skill comes from reading. Even if you are a math major and planning to take the MCAT for medical school, you need to take at least one elective that requires you to read several books during the term. The more you read (and write), the better you score on these tests. Fun and funky courses in contemporary literature, poetry, or culture are often offered—later in your life and career you probably won't have time to engage with these, but they might very well serve the purpose now.

If you are planning on law school, this is also a good time to meet with the advisors for **law school** about the process for applying. The prelaw advisor may have to create a **dean's letter** or other affirmation of your integrity and fitness for law school—many schools require such documents. So get to know this person early. The advisor can also tell you about moot court or LSAT prep classes or internships with local law firms.

If you are considering off-campus programs, junior year is generally the best one in which to venture away from campus—to **study abroad**, do legislative internships, or take advantage of other credit-bearing experiences that further your goals. In your sophomore year you are still dealing with required courses and making decisions about direction; in your senior year you want to be on hand for job or graduate program interviews. So junior year is perfect for these off-campus experiences

Your career chances are greatly enhanced by having experiences on your résumé that make you stand out. (If you're interested in the path to the CEO's office, it now usually has a stop in a foreign posting.) Studying abroad is an invaluable experience to venture forth, build your language skills, broaden your cultural exposure, and take some risks. And your tuition for approved programs abroad is likely the same as you're paying now, or even less. You must make arrangements with the bursar or financial aid offices, as well as work with an advisor to plan and get pre-approval for the program and course choices for your study abroad. Time away is *not* something you launch into on your own. Working with the designated office at your school, you plan your time away.

You may have the choice of living in a dorm or with a family. There are pros and cons to each. Living with a family, if harmonious, can give you more language practice, insight into local culture, and lasting relationships. A dorm may feel safer and more like your life at home, but you do end up with other students just like you, unless you find other ways to engage with the local scene. Most schools abroad have different schedules from ours, which may allow for more free time to travel to other cities or countries near your home base. You can travel relatively inexpensively using rail passes and living in hostels.

Over the years I have loved the cards, gifts, and emails I've gotten from students from Australia to Argentina. No one has ever returned and said he did not learn an enormous amount from the experience. Most have said study abroad was a transformative experience, and many have redirected their life plans as a result of it.

Junior year is also an ideal time to engage in **internships**. You are now at the stage where you're thinking ahead to career goals, and you want to give them a test drive. You may be able to do an internship during the school year for a few hours a week (no more than fifteen). Or you can do an internship during the summer before either your junior year or, more typically, your senior year. The career office can provide many lists of openings, and recruiters looking for interns may be on campus, representing corporations or not-for-profits. While you won't get paid at a not-for-profit, the skills and contacts you gain are easily transferable to the for-profit sector. Job sites such as **www.idealist.org** or the careers section of the *Chronicle of*

Philanthropy can be helpful too. Also check the notices in your department and ask your advisor.

Internships solidify your sense of direction and knowledge of a field and help build your skills. They enhance your résumé and sometimes even lead to a job offer. They may come with credits instead of pay, though some may provide both a stipend and course credits. Earning credits would require producing a project, a journal, or a paper, for example, that both a faculty advisor and your site supervisor evaluate.

Internships are considered so valuable that some families are even paying for their children to have the experience. This is clearly not an option for most families. Your career office is your free ticket to finding an internship.

Some internship programs can take you away from your home campus during junior year. There are credit-bearing federal and state internship programs that sometimes struggle to find students—especially students in underrepresented minorities. These include internships with federal or state legislators or other public figures, and even in the White House. For your law school application, certainly an internship at your state house or in Washington looks wonderful. Other campuses offer exchange programs. For example, historically Black colleges and universities (HBCUs) such as Spelman College in Atlanta, provide a distinct culture and view of society. Talk to your advisors to see what is possible and right for you.

Junior year is an optimum time to solidify and enrich your experiences and your plans for the future—a rich preparation year for what is to come.

SENIOR YEAR

In your senior year you are taking the steps toward your longer-term future. It can be both an intensely busy and highly emotional year. You may be preparing grad school applications while taking a full courseload and spending hours with friends you fear you'll never see again.

If you've done most things right in the previous three years, you'll be on track for a successful senior year. But in any case, it's not a bad idea to start out with a checklist to make sure you are taking care of everything, because halfway through the term may be too late.

A Checklist

- ☐ Check your school's process for ensuring that you are on track and on time to meet all the degree requirements (you usually find the requirements online). You may need a signoff by a dean or advisor. Have you met all the requirements, both general and for your majors/minors? If not, what can you do now to meet them? (My college actually used to require a swimming test for graduation!)
- ☐ Are your library late charges paid?
- ☐ Are there any incompletes on your record?
- ☐ Do you have a strong résumé that has been vetted by the career office staff?
- ☐ Be sure that you have spoken to your faculty about recommendations you may need for grad school or other applications. If you're among the lucky ones eligible to apply for the Rhodes, Marshall, Gates, or Fulbright fellowships (or other prestigious postgraduate fellowships), the deadlines are often in early fall of your senior year. Warn your professors the spring or summer before that you need letters from them as early as September.
- ☐ Are there application deadlines for job interviews or job fairs?
- ☐ What is the deadline for applying to graduate?

Usually there is a section of your college website with all the information about graduation. A special week may be set aside for senior pictures and for ordering your academic robes and rings. There may also be an advisor focused on seniors' needs.

One consideration should be financial planning. Application fees for grad schools hit in the fall. Later in the year, you may want to order the class ring, contribute to a class gift, order graduation pictures, rent cap and gown, and attend parties or proms. All of this is pricey, and you need to budget for it.

Graduate school application fees can be more than a hundred dollars each, though if you are below a certain income level or participated in a program such as the McNair, you may be eligible for fee waivers or reductions.

End Results

The senior year varies from fall to spring semester.

The fall, frankly, can be pretty tense. You will be applying for your next step after college in the fall or a semester before you complete your degree, not in the week before graduation. (Actually, you should have been working on this all along!) The offices that handle these matters are all geared up to work with you as soon as you arrive in the fall, or as soon as you hit the credit level that marks you as a senior.

What are you applying for? Typically, you have four categories of choices:

- Graduate schools, including professional schools—law, medicine, or business
- Special fellowships that may fund some of your graduate education options or offer new ones—Rhodes, Marshall, Fulbright, Gates, Jack Kent Cooke, Ford, National Science Foundation, and others
- Jobs in areas you've prepared for specifically as an undergraduate— film, teaching, social work, or other fields that fit the skills and interests you've developed through your liberal arts background
- Special programs—Teach for America, the Peace Corps, or AmeriCorps. For some students, such as those looking at high medical school bills, the military may also offer an option.

All of these are competitive. During the summer before your senior year, look at these options and see which might fit you best (not fit your parents, but you). Then talk frankly with the advisor or office familiar with these matters and the advisor who best knows you. There is also an excellent website for graduate school admissions questions: **www.gradschool.about.com**. It is better to be in the running than not, if you meet the basic criteria. In your senior year you will be applying for something.

All of this activity requires organization. Look at the deadlines and work backward to see what you have to do to prepare personal statements, get recommendations, and polish your résumé. Ideally, you should get all of this done a few days before the deadlines to allow for the inevitable disaster that strikes (the professor gets the flu when your letter is due, the computer dies...). Be sure to back up all your personal statements and other key documents. We get lazy about this, but a glitch can undo all your plans. And be sure that the statement or letter meant for UCLA does not say you are wild about Wash U. This is the kind of mistake that comes from being tense and rushed.

Besides applications and stressful decision making, at some schools you may be engaged in research for a **thesis, honors paper, or capstone project**. Any of these represents the pinnacle of your undergraduate academic experience. This type of project allows you to work independently in an area of your own passion and expertise. Usually a document or paper of significant length is required, and typically you are mentored or advised by a professor in your field. It is usually due at the end of the year, although you may have identified the topic in your junior year and worked on it all of your senior year.

This is your chance to pull together what you've learned about the subject you've chosen, and to apply your research and writing skills. It should be a subject you really love, because you spend so much time with it. And it may even be the beginning of a career if you embrace scholarly work or advocacy as a career path.

Don't forget to breathe. Yes, you are working hard at all of these activities while trying to sustain a high GPA in the classes you have remaining. Sleep does not seem like much of an option. But you do need to sleep, and continue to exercise and spend time with friends. Long conversations late at night in a lounge or coffee shop seem very important with these classmates you did not know just a few years before and who are now among the most important persons in your life. Indeed, this may be the last time you have to connect with some of them, other than online. Some will remain or move in and out of your life as you move around in career, geography, or just life. So value this time with them.

B Plans

Senior year is full of highs and lows. You don't get into every school or program you apply for, or you get into some, but not with the funding you hoped for. Your friends help you celebrate the highs and console you through the lows. If you're accepted for the job, fellowship, grad program, or project, then you can both celebrate and relax somewhat. You still need to keep up the GPA and finish the research project.

Waiting to hear can be *very* stressful. You just want to know one way or the other if you are in or out of the running. Once you know, you can move ahead, maybe even to a plan B. (Always have a plan B!)

If you have options, you have to make choices. And if you did not do as well in your quest as you hoped, you activate plan B. What can plan B look like? When you choose to apply to grad schools, for instance, be sure there is a range, including one "reach" school and one "safe." The safe school is plan B. It may not be ideal, but should have enough favorable features that you will not be unhappy there. It may be located in a place you had not considered, or not have the perfect professor you dreamed of working with, or it may be smaller or larger than you envisioned, but it could be just fine.

A really good plan B is to take a year off between college and graduate or professional school. The reality is that business schools do not want to see you until you've worked for two years anyway, and law schools tend in that direction also. That way you enter grad school with some actual experience to bring to the classroom. Clearing your head for a bit and actually trying out the field you're considering before you take the plunge may be a smart move. Some say that mature students in graduate programs are more focused and complete the degrees faster.

Sometimes during your time off, life takes you in a totally different direction. Two of my own children talked about law school; one is now a marketing consultant and the other a fund-raiser. Neither would have been happy with law school, and both love the work they do. They found that out only by being in the workplace first.

So, plan B is to line up a job at the same time you're doing grad school applications. Then you may have to make a choice. You get a great job offer and a great grad school offer—toss a coin and see what your heart says while it is in the air.

A Story: Allen

Allen was brilliant. He had a 3.9 GPA, with a major in British literature. As a Black person, he was underrepresented in the field, and many programs considered him a potential asset and sought him out. But he was not sure of his direction. He got an offer from Goldman Sachs, then a prominent financial services firm, for their management training program. Though he was not a finance or economics major, his GPA said that he was smart, and his major said he had strong writing skills. He spent two years at the firm and was set to get an offer, including a stipend, for an MBA program. But after the two years he knew that he did not love the business world. He had, though, developed an interest in law and went on to earn his degree in that field. He is now a professor at a prestigious law school. He would not have suspected that would be a path for him had he not had a shot at the corporate world first. And his earnings at Goldman allowed him to go to law school without incurring a big debt!

Another plan B is to apply for a job or grad school along with a program like the Peace Corps or Teach for America. Take yourself totally out of your comfort zone and into a real-life adventure where you may engage in work that not only changes your life but also the lives of others. You may discover strengths and resilience beyond what you expected. These are good options for you now especially as you do not, in most cases, have a family or a mortgage, but instead are footloose and fancy free.

A Story: Kathy

Kathy came from a largely homogeneous, white upper-class background and attended a similarly populated college not far from home. She was not sure of her goals after college, but she was smart and plucky.

She was accepted into the Teach for America program and sent to Phoenix, Arizona. There she taught fifth-grade Latino children and found that they could not read well. She took it upon herself to learn how to raise money and created a reading program for her students. Along the way she and her roommate became foster parents for two children whose parents were incarcerated.

Kathy lived a life she had never imagined and used skills she never knew she had. She went on to earn a graduate degree in educational counseling and to stay involved in education. Based on her experiences as a young woman, she now works hard to assure that her own children are aware of the many different kinds of lives Americans lead.

A plan B can be a life changer. It also helps to relieve the stress of banking on one particular outcome.

By second semester you have an idea of what lies ahead, at least in terms of an action plan. You need to concentrate on that final paper or project. You may have comprehensive exams in your major or as part of an honors program.

Yet while you still need to keep your eye on the ball academically, you can relax a bit and enjoy the moment, and even begin to bask in memories with your friends. But don't go overboard. By getting drunk and disorderly, you can trash your plans before they even begin, with just one tacky picture on Facebook or one tragic accident. Senior pub crawls may be a tradition, but they are not a good idea. You have seen the stories and read the headlines—I do not need to say more.

As you sprint toward the finish line of graduation, there is no question that you have had crises along the way and that someone has pulled you out of the soup. This is the time to have long talks with your favorite professors and to thank them and anyone else who has been particularly helpful along the way.

Chapter 8
TIME MANAGEMENT AND STUDY SKILLS

MANAGING YOUR TIME

Did you know it's recommended that you study 2 hours for every credit hour you take? So if you're taking 16 credits, that's 32 hours of study a week. But you're working 20 hours a week. And you commute 3 hours each day, totalling 21 hours a week. And you do need to sleep at least 6 hours (42 per week) or you're a mess. That's 115 hours a week accounted for right there. And that's only with minimal sleep. Students who sleep more do better by a significant degree, according to a recent study reported in *Time* magazine (December 7, 2009). Psychologists from Hendrix University in Arkansas and researchers from the University of Pittsburgh found that lack of sleep has an impact on GPA.

There's obviously not enough time in the day. We all say that at some point, sometimes frequently. But actually, depending on how we choose to use it, there *is* enough time. I know perfectly well that if I watched less TV I would get more done of a productive nature—I make a choice though. Less time on Facebook or YouTube, less beer drinking, playing Frisbee or guitar, commenting on *American Idol*, or hanging out at Starbucks—less of all of those could yield you more time, too. The activities listed in the first paragraph above total 115 hours, but there are 168 hours in a week. It's up to you how you spend the remaining 53, which equals more than 7 hours every day—fooling around or doing laundry, attending a club meeting, dating, seeing a movie, or whatever else you want or need to do.

A Cautionary Tale: Liza and Her Late Paper

Liza was intimidated by her Spanish professor and put off doing her paper for his course until it was nearly too late to get it in. She let her fear of failure keep her from talking to the instructor, let alone getting the work done. She finally, at her roommate's urging, talked to an advisor, who helped get communication going between Liza and her instructor, so she could confront the source of her fear and paralysis. Liza finished the course with a solid B grade.

Lessons learned: Don't wait until you're down to the wire to seek support. Be sure you allow enough time to get your work done.

To be more productive, the first thing you need to do is determine your **time management style**. This may seem annoying, but it is really useful. For one week write down everything you do and how long it takes; do this with a friend, to compare notes and make getting it done more likely. I know, for example, that it takes me exactly two hours to brush my teeth, feed the dog, exercise, have breakfast, shower, dress, and walk the dog, before I sit down at my computer to start work. How long do morning preparations take you? Also, note how long it takes to get to school, to classes, to have lunch, to study, and to do whatever else needs doing, for the entire day. I bet you find surprises by the time the week ends.

If you work longer hours or have a family to care for, then your time is more constrained (and perhaps more unpredictable). But students do manage all of these things *and* school. Often, paradoxically, those who have more to do are more effective and do better in school—and often in life.

A Student's Strategy: Endri Horanilli, Hunter College '08, Research Coordinator, Sloan-Kettering Hospital

My mom was the main reason I was somewhat organized when I was in college. She showed me time and time again that it is easier to do things as they came up, rather than putting them off. So often when I had papers to do, she would push me to do them earlier, so I would have more time for other activities, which was great advice.

I found out while I was going to school, working, and being a teaching assistant all at the same time (the busiest I was during those years) that the more things I had to do, the better it was for me to stay on top of everything. The fewer things I had to do, the more bored I became—perhaps intellectually—I have yet to figure this out. In a way, it makes sense to me, because I would have been prone to procrastination if I had few things to do and distant deadlines. Having many responsibilities forced me to categorize tasks in order of importance and tackle them one by one until they were all finished.

Once you know where your time is spent, you can make your schedule work more effectively for you. The best strategy is to **plan**. That means you need some tools—a planner, a PDA, a calendar. I myself prefer a Google calendar and lots of lists and Post-it sticky notes. Use whatever works best for you—and I emphasize *use*.

Planning is not simply recording when you have a dinner date or a paper due. It involves looking ahead and also back. You look ahead to see, for example, when your paper is due, then look back to see where you have blocks of time to work on the paper. You should put tasks requiring long stretches of time, such as writing, in time blocks of an hour or more. Set a goal for a first draft and put that on your calendar. Make a date to show the draft to your professor. You not only impress your teacher, but keep yourself from procrastinating.

Other assignments, such as reading a novel for your literature class, may be done in small time chunks. Always have that book with you for the times when you're on the bus to school or in line at the grocery, or just have some moments available. But do put the reading on your to-do list for the day.

A Student's Strategy: Opal Hope Bennett, New York University '98, Attorney

My best practices for time management while in school involved having the right plan and the right tools.

The Plan

- Always record your obligations in a space where you can see them all at one time (for example, syllabus assignments; committee meetings; Aunt Sally's birthday).
- Take the time to plan out a to-do list that covers a week, a month, and a semester at a time.
- Only use a plan to the extent that it helps; don't obsess over it.
- Don't overload yourself by taking on too many obligations. Always keep your principal endeavor first. Always make time for play.

The Tools

- I used a desk blotter calendar that I mounted on my wall, and I had four different color markers for four categories of activities: Personal, Class, Extracurricular, and Assignments/Deadlines.
- A day planner is essential.

Let's discuss the **to-do list**. Keep a daily list of the main tasks you want or need to accomplish that day. You're less likely to forget them that way. If you spend two hours working on your lab report, you know you're that much ahead for the next day, even if the report is still incomplete. Try this for a couple of days, and see if you don't feel a little more proud of yourself when, at the end of the day, you can see "done" items crossed out. Sometimes you need to make the list come to life—set reminders in your calendar or PDA, or put stickies on your mirror. You can even ask friends to remind you to check your list, as you work on getting used to using it.

Don't beat yourself up if you don't get everything done. Situations can interfere—illness, a child's needs, a new priority at work. A good plan allows some wiggle room. Allow extra time for travel or to get to and from classes or meetings, since you never know when traffic will be ugly, you will encounter friends, or the elevators will be slow. This is realistic planning. You feel better if you're always a bit early, as opposed to always a little late. Being late is rude and stressful. Think also how you hate it when you're cooling your heals in the doctor's office. Think how you feel when you're rushed and apologetic for your lateness. Planning allows you to slow down; it is healthier. Move an item to the next day if you can't get to it. But if you have to keep moving items, it's an indication of a time-management problem, and you should stop to see what's happening.

One of the biggest factors interfering with a plan is fear. Really. You may be afraid you can't write a paper, and so you put it off. It's better to talk about matters making you anxious than to be paralyzed by the fear of them. Fear can also relate to not being able to **say no**. Out of fear of being unpopular, you agree to go to a party you have no time for, chair a committee you have no time for, or hang out when you know you should be studying or working. Although Nancy Reagan's once famous advice, "Just say no," didn't work in getting drug use down, it works for time management. You can effectively say "no" by saying that you're sorry but you have other plans, or are just swamped. You don't have to explain more than that. You can look at your PDA and shake your head as you say, "Sorry, too busy."

Besides, if you're that busy, you must be popular or worth spending time with. The students who are always available may be the ones with unsatisfactory lives—not who you want to be. You want to be the person with clear priorities, and that includes planning time for yourself. A nap means you *are* busy, as does the gym. It is not a waste of time. Time you lose being in the infirmary because you got sick from lack of sleep or food or exercise is *really* time wasted.

A Student's Strategy: Meadow Braun, New York University '98, Arts Educator

Test Your Limits
Take on more than you think you can handle. The fuller your schedule, the more value you will place on your time. You'll find yourself becoming more efficient out of necessity and will be surprised at how capable you are.

Keep a Calendar or Planner
Maintain an up-to-date calendar or planner and keep it handy at all times. Refer to it often throughout the day to keep yourself on track. If you have a deadline on Wednesday, enter a reminder for Tuesday, so you're not scrambling at the last minute.

Make Lists
Keep a list of things to do, things to buy, people to call, etc. Draw a box or a line to the left of each one so that you can enjoy the satisfaction of checking it off when completed. Make gratuitous use of your highlighter! Break your lists down into whatever categories work for you (i.e., by class, order of importance, and so forth).

Make Your Health a Priority
Allow time to focus on your personal health and well-being every day. It's just as important as any final exam or interview, so go ahead and write it into your schedule! Healthy diet and exercise, relaxation,

time with friends, time alone, and plenty of sleep are just some of the elements that can help ensure you have the inner resources to tackle your busy schedule without burning out.

Be Creative

Find creative ways to accomplish multiple tasks at once, for example, study while eating lunch in the park or working out at the gym. Think about the physical map of your day and try to organize your activities in a logical and time-efficient order. Never underestimate the power of a few minutes—reading a couple of pages here and there throughout the day can get you through a whole chapter more quickly than you thought.

Make achieving your goals a communal activity. Let someone else know your short-term goals. If you're determined to have your lab report done by Thursday so you can enjoy your weekend, tell a friend. If you have to get grad school applications in by November 1, tell your mentor or advisor. If you need to be up early to exercise, find an exercise buddy. Others can help you stay focused and resist tempting distractions. They might even say no for you. A student I knew was teaching while earning her master's degree. Her young students knew she had to take tests and do papers as they did, and they would ask if she had done her homework too.

Setting **priorities** means you have to think about the long term. Why are you in college? You are there to gain the skills and credentials that will help your dreams come true. You are not there to drink the most beer, be president of the sorority, direct every play on campus, or win the Final Four in basketball. Your classwork, the job that allows you to stay in school or furthers your career plans, your health, and your relationships are your priorities. The balance can shift periodically, but you have to keep those four in your sights at all times.

Think in terms of two concepts: **balance and imperfection**. The first means no one thing takes over your life at the expense of others important to you. The second refers to allowing yourself to be somewhat imperfect. You want your paper to be the best you can do, but revising it twelve times and citing thirty-six sources is excessive and may not get you what you want after all. An A or B+ is fine, an A+ is gravy. It's all right to get three A's and a B. Of course you should try hard, but accept limitations on your capacities and your time. You are not in school because you're perfect, but because you are, and will always be, still learning. Think of your goal as making good progress, not achieving perfection. Many students put too much pressure on themselves, spending time on tasks and activities that are not important in the long term. Keeping these in balance and giving them your best, using all the tools you have at hand, should keep you sane and healthy.

A Student's Strategy: Robert Accordino, Princeton University '03, Medical Student; Founder, Music for Autism

During my early college days, I remember feeling that while, compared to high school, I was in class fewer hours each week, I had a lot more to do for classes in the context of a less structured day. I piled on a ton of extracurricular activities—from joining an a cappella singing group, to serving as a member of the Student Health Advisory Board, to being a Big Brother to a local teenager, to tutoring chemistry at a local high school.

The principle I tried to follow in high school remained true for me at the start of college: to get a variety of tasks accomplished in a day, I had to try to focus only on that activity as I was doing it. For example, when I had to work through a problem set for my biology course, I couldn't start thinking about the song I had to learn for my a cappella group, or everything would take longer, and I would just wind up wasting time. Similarly, if during my a cappella group rehearsals, which occurred five nights a week, I would start getting stressed about an upcoming introductory psychology exam, I would immediately try to stop myself from doing this. I think being strict with myself about my level of concentration on a particular task has been tremendously important to my time management.

MULTITASK

Read on your way to school (if you're not driving). Read in the laundry room. Pay bills while you watch TV. Meet your boyfriend in the library and then have coffee afterward. Do an internship for credit so you get both the course credit and the experience. Look for jobs that have lots of down time—I've known many students who took security jobs so they could study while at work or who worked in the library during relatively quiet times. Be creative in figuring out how you can combine tasks without sacrificing the quality of either one.

Note: texting during class does not count as productive activity. You cannot tweet, text, or chat while studying or listening to a lecture and expect to get anything from it. Though some multitasking is useful (in the situations I describe above, there is little if any conflict), some tasks take away from your productivity when combined—even your safety, such as texting while driving. Recent studies show, in fact, that our many technological devices prevent us from being able to focus, and thus hinder us from doing anything really well. Use technology as a tool that you control, not the other way around.

Sometimes **competing priorities** create pressure. What if you're the star of the basketball team or en route to the Olympics, or have been offered the chance to dance for a major company or act in a film or play that is career making? In these cases, the big winners stick with school and work out a schedule that may mean taking longer to graduate or taking a leave of absence, but they do not give up on their education altogether. Michael Jordan has a degree from the University of North Carolina at Chapel Hill, and as a retiree from basketball, he has his education to draw on as a successful businessman. Jennifer Connelly, the actor, is a Yale graduate, and

Natalie Portman was a Hollywood star while still at Harvard. Your coaches, professors, and deans can help you plan a strategy that allows you to embrace your talent while continuing to advance your college career. Sometimes a leave is required, but always plan to come back.

A Story: Alice

In her junior year, Alice, a talented ballerina, was offered the chance to dance with the American Ballet Theater company. It was a once-in-a-lifetime opportunity, and she discussed it with her advisor. The advisor helped Alice weigh the pros and cons, and they agreed that Alice should go ahead and take the offer, even though it would make college life impossible because of the travel.

After a year, Alice injured her knee and could no longer dance. She returned to college, took up a major in economics, and then became a financial consultant.

Alice is glad to have been able to experience the best of both worlds.

STUDY TIPS

Getting good grades is essential to your achieving your goals. Your grades may be critical to holding on to a scholarship or to getting one. Many students think that if they just go over and over the material that will suffice. But the reality is that study is an art. Each discipline needs to be approached differently and every student learns differently. So putting those two together in a way that works best for you will assure the outcomes you want and need.

Let's go back to the idea of planning and think about your classes. Which ones are easy for you? Perhaps you love the subject, the material just comes easily to you, or there is not a lot of work required. Now think about the ones that are difficult. The subject takes a lot of effort; the professor assigns a ton of work; you would avoid the course if it weren't required.

You typically approach the easy ones with a more positive attitude and a willingness to tackle them first. *That is the wrong strategy.* Figure out how much time you need to do the work of your hardest classes and then align that work with when you are freshest and most alert and able to focus. Do that work first. Hold out the work you enjoy for last—make it dessert.

I must confess that when grading papers I knew that some would be painful and need much work, and some would be a delight. I put the latter at the bottom of the pile—they were a reward. This way you can get the double reward of getting a difficult task out of the way and then tackling a pleasurable one, the lab work or reading you were looking forward to.

Considering again the courses that take more effort, think about what elements are hard for you. If you're not a good writer, for instance, then plan to spend time with your professor and in the writing center, and also have a friend look over your drafts. You therefore must have a longer planning horizon for writing papers. Mark your calendar with those factors in mind.

Find a **study space**. Learn where and under what conditions you study best. Some students need total silence, so the library or their dorm room may work. If you've always studied with some level of background noise—your family is noisy, you live near a highway—or you drown out background noises like truck traffic by listening to music, then you may want to create or find study space that has some amount of ambient noise. Your iPod might serve the purpose. If your room or apartment is too distracting—the TV and the bed tempt you—then find somewhere else. Possible choices include the library or an empty classroom. I actually used to climb a tree outside my dorm to study in good weather. In any case, whatever works for you is fine, but unlike my tree, where I could really only read, your space should ideally allow you to have all your tools at hand—your notes, laptop, texts.

This next tip may surprise you. **Learn how to read.** Yes, you made it to college, so you likely know how to read. But that does not mean you know how to *really* read—where it is more about comprehension and interpretation. I cannot stress enough the importance of understanding what you're reading. Plowing through and turning pages when you don't get it does not make sense and wastes time. Stop and ask an upperclassman, a brilliant class-mate, a TA, or your professor, if necessary. I have seen far too many students sit silently, not understanding a word of what is going on, and then blow the test, midterm, or paper.

If you're reading in the humanities or social sciences, you're looking for themes or key concepts, and evidence to support them. How does the author make her case? Look at the table of contents and even the index of a book, or at the introduction of an essay as the roadmap to where the author wants to lead you. Unlike when reading a mystery novel, it is okay to jump to the end to see what the conclusion is likely to be. Then read the middle, looking for the proofs and examples of what the author wants you to believe or understand. Once you know what you're looking for, you can skim or read faster. Make note if you disagree with the author's premises and why. Use whatever tools work for you to highlight key points. Underline, take notes, or mark a page with a Post-it note.

Some types of writing require close reading. Poetry demands careful read-ing, as, in that form, meanings are likely to be more subtly conveyed. If you are majoring in literature, it is assumed that you love to read, since you'll do so much of it. And as you home in on a text, you are also looking for concepts. Close reading shows how the writer uses language, and conceptual reading reveals the themes.

Science writing conveys facts and process, and it is usually more concise. You have to know (often memorize) and understand the material, and be able to explain it clearly and cogently. Sometimes it helps to try to explain material to someone not familiar with it as a way of testing your own understanding. Students who tutor often find it useful practice for their own learning processes.

When reading in an unfamiliar or difficult field, it helps if you ask your-self why the material is important and relevant. Understanding genes, for instance, may have relevance to your own health. The ancient Greek comedy *Lysistrata* deals with women's attitudes toward war when husbands and sons go off and may never return, and this is a theme as relevant now as it was then. No matter what you're reading, think about its importance and that will help you engage with the reading

Here is the key point about **studying**: Find the big or most important ideas in whatever you're working on. It may be a concept, formula, or series of facts. If you mark up a text (one you own and do not plan to sell later) or take notes, do *not* write down or underline everything—just the *big* ideas, those you *must* know. Underline words, not paragraphs (the exception is if you plan to quote a paragraph in a paper later; then I would just note it with a sticky, or bookmark it in your computer). Ask your professor what the most important concepts are, what you're expected to master. (Do not ask what will be on the test—that is tacky and does not play well to the professor.)

Devise your own tools to help you retain material. You can make flash cards and carry them around to memorize formulas or vocabulary. Make notes in the margins of your class notes. (If you keep notes on your laptop, print them out so you can review them in your multitasking mode.) Keep an online diary for each class, where you record the key concepts you're learning as you go, and how they hang together. Develop a one-page summary of that week's material. If you're a visual learner, make diagrams or pictures to help you remember material. It's another way of summarizing. If you find that you can't summarize, it is a sign you have not learned or understood the material.

If math, science, or another subject is hard for you, seek out the professor, the TA, or a tutor (or all three). Look at the most successful students, and you'll see they are not going it alone. Your school may allow you to access resources such as **www.askonline.net**, which provides online tutoring, often using tutors from your own campus. Some subjects, often quantitative, lend themselves to the use of **study groups**. Lab work is often done in teams. Successful students form groups to solve problems or test themselves, and they share strengths or different ways of framing the work so it is clearer. I know one student who used to frame positive and negative ions in chemistry in terms of sex, which certainly made the concepts memorable. Remember, it's acceptable to help other students understand how to get an answer, but not to give them the answer. That is cheating, and those persons then don't learn the concepts, so they could lose in two ways. By teaching someone else, however, we reinforce our own learning.

I can't stress enough how important it is to **go to class**. I remember the student who turned up at my office concerned that he had failed the midterm. It turned out he had not been coming to class. A few weeks later he stopped by to say what a difference attending class had made in his grades!

Not only that, but some professors note your class absences. Some, especially in courses where knowledge is a building process, tolerate only three or four unexcused absences before you get an automatic F. (Note the word "unexcused"—if you are ill, required to work, have a death in the family and can provide evidence of your issue, take it to the instructor, ideally in advance, but at least as soon as possible.) This policy will usually be spelled out explicitly in the syllabus. Languages, math, and biology may be among the subjects that require attendance. They are essential courses that can affect the rest of your college career.

Next, when in class turn off your iPod, cell phone, and BlackBerry, and use your laptop only to take notes, not surf the Web. Some professors are now banning electronic media in the classroom altogether because of the distraction.

Yes, it's true that some professors may drone. I had one who put himself to sleep in his own lectures! I still had to get a grade, though, and learning the material and what he considered important was essential. The best teachers are lively, engaging, and comprehensible, but that brings its own challenges to note-taking. Similar to taking notes from your readings, you need to capture their most important points, not their every word.

Find ways to make your note-taking interesting. Students I've known used different ink or pen colors for different ideas (turquoise on green paper, brown ink on tan; concepts in blue, formulas in red). Figure out a shorthand for taking notes (your experience with texting will help here). The process helps you remember. You can also mark up your notes to clarify them or enhance your retention of the material.

Any exercises done in class are meant to convey a point and signal you to pay attention. Questions about the reading (which the instructor assumes you've done) give you a clue as to what's important and may show up on an exam or be expected in a final paper. Class discussion, especially in a small group or seminar, can help you understand the material, but also allows you to show off what you know. You may even get a lively discussion or dispute going if the topic is hot enough. Points for class participation come in here. It is expected that you have done the homework so you can engage intelligently. Frankly, it's embarrassing for all if you're called on and fumble around or have nothing to say because you did not do the assigned work. Professors spend hours every week preparing their lectures or course content. They plan the material to be covered and how skills can be learned. They're invested in increasing your knowledge and competence. This is a partnership wherein you have to do your share too.

The places where you have to show what you know are **tests and papers**. Going back to the planning idea, be sure that you plan enough preparation time for these. Deep study, research, and writing require big chunks of time. At the end of the process, review or editing can be done with smaller chunks. An adrenaline rush may come from waiting until the last minute, but that does not work in every case. You should definitely not plan to cram for all your exams. For sure, do not gamble on cramming for the one in your hardest class or the one you're most anxious about. Sometimes you're lucky to have a professor who requires many quizzes or short papers during the term. These are annoying at first, but they can save you in the end, as you're able to gauge where you are along the way, rather than procrastinating until the end. And your grade doesn't depend on one or two big items like a final exam or paper. Since you have a concrete idea of how you're doing as you go, you can take action as needed.

To **prepare for tests,** there are a few things to do first. Find out what to expect—the unknown is often most scary, and if you can figure out what's coming, you're on more solid emotional ground. Sometimes the professor helpfully tells you what types of questions are on an exam and maybe even provides study sessions. Sometimes you have to guess, based on other tests given in class. Sometimes you can get copies of past exams on file in the department office or library, or from the professor. And sometimes a former student from the class can give you an idea of what to expect.

After you know what to expect, decide if you should study with a group or partner. Organize your material. Get your notes together, and rewrite or summarize the items you have marked in any texts or materials you've read.

Info: Study Guides

Rather than take time here with detailed strategies for studying specific subjects, I want to refer you to a couple of resources I think do a good job on this front. One is the website **http://how-to-study.com**. The other two are books: *What Smart Students Know: Maximum Grades. Optimum Learning. Minimum Time.* by Adam Robinson, a cofounder of *Princeton Review*; the other is Ron Fry's *How to Study*. There are certainly more books on the subject, and often your own campus will have workshops, websites, and guides of its own.

The biggest mistake students make in the exam room (sometimes while sleep-deprived) is misreading the questions. You may be rushing—stop, breathe, and read carefully, to be sure you know exactly what's being sought. If there is room for interpretation, go with the sense that most closely reflects the viewpoint the professor has focused on all term (another reason to go to classes). If there are several questions, first do those you know, to build your confidence, then tackle the ones you may struggle over. If you don't complete all, you at least know you've done a good job on the parts you know.

If you finish the test early, don't just put down your pen and run from the room. Being done early gives you time to go back and check your answers or expand on some, if that's appropriate. You'd be quite vexed with yourself if you lost points on a silly error that you could have caught on review.

A Cautionary Tale:
Merisa and the Missed Test Question

Merisa was doing just fine in her courses, on her way to a solid B+ or even an A average. She was sailing through one of her final exams, sure she would ace it. When she handed it in, she noted with some pride that she had finished first.

When she got her grade, she was shocked to find that she had failed the test. In tears, she went to see the instructor, who asked why she had not completed the exam. Merisa had not seen the last question, which was on the back of the questions page (as the environmentally conscious professor had used both sides of the paper). The other class members took more time to complete the test because they had read the entire exam first.

Fortunately, since the professor knew the caliber of Merisa's work, he allowed her to take a make-up exam, which saved her academic record from being seriously damaged. Merisa was lucky, as many faculty members would not have been so generous.

Lessons learned: Read and understand all test questions, and review your work before you consider yourself done. Being the first one finished may not be such a good thing.

When **writing a paper**, begin by discussing your topic with your professor. He or she can be a remarkable source of clarification of your topic and source material. One professor teaching freshman English told her students that they could submit their papers to her in English, French, Spanish, Italian, Greek, or Latin, as she read all of these languages. Though she was scary smart, the main point is she also was able to give her students excellent guidance on the books and other resources necessary to do their papers, as well as direction on how to organize them.

A conversation with your professor ensures that you are on the right track.

Some professors allow you to submit drafts, and you should take them up on the offer. Some even assign drafts as homework, so you can't get caught at the last minute with nothing to show.

Next, go to the library and/or the Web (not Wikipedia) to find source material. The librarian is your new best friend, who, like your professors, can lead you to source material.

Then you need to think. Think about what you want to say or prove in the paper. You have discussed it with your instructor, but now you are thinking more about how you want to make your points. That leads you to an **outline**, which is really crucial. It will force you to organize your thoughts and your material.

Begin with the introduction, which spells out what you plan to prove or demonstrate—your argument. The body of the paper should be broken up into several parts, in which you provide evidence for the case you're building or the story you're telling. The conclusion summarizes your findings and may suggest that there is more work to be done in the field, or offer recommendations, or simply conclude that you proved what you set out to do. An outline doesn't need to be more than a page. In the middle section I've always made notes of the texts or other evidence I plan to use. I'd have stacks of books set up around my study or room, organized by the section of the outline they pertained to—and God help the person who moved a stack!

Next, using your outline, write a **rough draft**. This gets your basic thoughts down fast; you go back and refine later. Actually, if you've allowed yourself enough time, you can do a couple of drafts. Whatever you do, do *not* submit the first draft. It will rarely be your best work.

If **English is not your first language**, be sure to have someone else from the writing center or a friend who is strong in English also look at your work. Again, this takes planning, because these extra reviews take time. Others have deadlines of their own.

Not all professors note your grammatical errors, but they may well reduce your grade because of them. Please pay attention to grammar and spelling. Having grammar and spell-check on computers makes sloppiness of that kind less forgivable these days. But note that these computer aids don't always pick up usage errors. For example, spell-check can read both "their" and "there" as correct spellings, but they are not used the same way. Nothing is more frustrating to a professor than reading a paper that has good ideas but is badly written. Remember that good writing is one of the key skills you should take away from college to the workplace. Every paper is a chance to practice that skill.

Info: Deadlines

Faculty do not set deadlines arbitrarily. They are bound by deadlines too. For example, they have to turn in grades or report midterm problems by dates set by the deans or the registrar. They may actually get yelled at if they're late getting grades in!

If grades have to be submitted by a week before graduation to be sure that seniors are eligible to graduate (that is, they have passed all their classes), then a faculty member has little time to grade final papers and/or exams. Let's say your professor, who has a class of twenty-five, has assigned a fifteen-page final paper. That means she or he has 375 pages to read carefully and comment on, and then twenty-five records to review and calculate grades for. If you hand in your paper a day late, and your professor had a specific schedule to work on papers and figure final grades, you will have caused a delay in getting your paper graded as well as in the professor's ability to submit final grades on time. If the grades are **on a curve** (an averaging of all grades in a course), then you will have affected all your classmates. The professor could also claim that you had an unfair advantage in taking extra hours to do your work, compared to the rest of the class.

A caution:

If your professor asks you to email your paper, be sure to *keep a hard copy* of the paper as well as a copy of the transmittal record from your computer. While students once claimed that "the dog ate my homework," the claim that "the computer ate my paper" will be viewed with just as much suspicion. If your paper is late or not received, you will need to prove that it was done and sent on time.

Do not leave your paper under your teacher's door or in a mailbox or give it to a TA unless directed to do so by the professor. If that is the case, then contact the professor regarding where and when you left your work, to be sure that it is received in a timely fashion.

Some faculty even specify a time when a paper is due. In some cases it is midnight; in others it is 5 p.m., or noon. Ask—do not assume that midnight is the deadline.

Finally, learn from your mistakes. If you have grammatical errors in your first papers for freshman English, then learn how not to make those mistakes again. College is for learning, not for knowing everything as you walk in the door. We learn best, though most painfully, from our mistakes.

Be sure to get back papers or exams. If necessary, give the professor a self-addressed envelope, or arrange to pick up your work from the department assistant. I have always been amazed at the number of students who never pick up final papers that I've taken great pains to correct, in ways that could be useful to them.

Take every less-than-stellar paper or exam to your teacher and ask where you could have done better. You're not pleading for a do-over to get a better grade, but asking for a chance to learn how to improve. This is not an argument, but a teaching-learning moment between teacher and student. If you're sincere, it also serves you well as you build relationships with your instructors.

If you follow this approach, gradually every piece of work you do will be stronger. You're building your knowledge and skill base. This is also a good lesson for life.

Chapter 9
WHEN IT FEELS LIKE A CRISIS

We all have moments of panic and times of crisis and distress, when the problems in our lives seem insurmountable. And we all have times when we believe everyone else is smarter, more popular, more intelligent, more attractive, more together than we are. In college, you will encounter many such times. The key is to know how to handle them.

Those who handle these feelings and problems best we call resilient. They are not necessarily the headline makers. They have not been brought up with wealth, have not had perfect families, are not as gorgeous as Jennifer Lopez or Denzel Washington, but they manage to lead full lives, rich in friends and pride in work well done.

It is likely that you know many such individuals, and that they may, in fact, have inspired you. They may be the mothers, grandmothers, clergypersons, youth leaders, teachers, or family friends whom you come to respect and admire as you see what they've dealt with to become the worthy persons they are. There are also better-known individuals whose stories can be sources of inspiration for you. They may include pediatric neurosurgeon Dr. Ben Carson, whose story *Gifted Hands* was a TNT film, or Susan Boyle, who enjoyed wild success on *Britain's Got Talent*. The site **http://www.bronzeditions.com** features stories of Black achievers in particular. There are a variety of films about underdog sports teams or athletes, such as Ernie Davis in *The Extreme*. Writer Julia Alvarez's immigrant story, or those of astronauts Franklin Chang-Diaz or Ronald McNair, are inspiring. President Obama is also an obvious example.

No matter if they are famous or not, there are lessons to be learned from resilient people about how you can handle the challenging times you encounter along your college and life path. Keep some of your favorite stories close at hand for occasions when you need a lift and a reminder that others have overcome some of the same challenges and succeeded.

A Story: Alisha

Alisha was struggling with the volume of work she had to do. She did not know how to organize it or her time. Gradually she fell more and more behind. She became depressed and began to skip classes; finally, she did not leave her room. She did, however, heed a summons to the advising office and revealed to a sympathetic advisor how she was feeling and that she just wanted to sleep. The advisor got her to the learning center, where staff helped her learn to study effectively and efficiently and to see that she could even find time to read for fun. She also saw a counselor on campus to deal with the depression that had set in as a result of her fears. In the end she was a happy graduate.

The challenges you will encounter in college most likely come in these categories: academic, health and well-being, and personal-emotional. They may overlap, and they may come in bunches. There are often early warnings that you are encountering a problem—ranging from your own awareness of how you're feeling or behaving to signals from others, such as messages from the deans. The case might be that you can't register because your grades are too low or your bill is unpaid. When the administrators cannot get your attention one way, they find others. One is putting **a stop on your record**, which prevents your moving forward until you have met with someone official. The key is that when you are facing a problem, you need to take action to address it. Strategies and resources exist to handle each kind of problem you're likely to encounter. It's most essential not to try to carry a burden alone. Think once more of your "people" backing you up.

ACADEMIC CRISES

As we've pointed out in previous chapters, it is the rare student who walks into his first college class feeling fully confident. The rules are different in college—you are on your own to a much greater degree. Concerned with making a good first impression on both your instructor and your peers, you may sit quietly as though you understand it all. Remember, though, you're in college to learn, not to know it all. Being silent is not a good thing. It can lead to one of the first forms of academic crisis.

Being silent can cause significant academic crisis. Imagine you've been going along for several weeks, not really getting what's going on in class, and you're also having trouble understanding the readings. Since the knowledge in many fields—bio, economics, languages, and math—builds directly on what has gone before, the longer you wait to acknowledge your problems, the deeper in trouble you are. And you know it. But you assume that everyone else is just fine, and so you keep quiet in class. You don't want to show up at the tutoring center because it feels stigmatizing. You study for hours, reading the material over and over, though you don't understand it. Then you take the midterm—and fail it.

A Cautionary Tale: Fred's Secret

Fred felt in over his head from week one at his large research university, but told no one. He called home every week and fabricated stories of success. He continued to be seen on campus—in his dorm room, the cafeteria, and the student center—but stopped going to classes. When midterm reports on first-year students went to the dean's office, Fred was called in, but did not show up despite repeated entreaties.

By the second semester the school asked him to leave, much to his parents' shock. He ending up going to a small local college, where his family could keep an eye on him.

Lessons learned: *You can't hide out when you're in trouble. The school will eventually discover your situation, and there will be consequences.*

Hiding is not a strategy. As soon as you feel overwhelmed by your work, find help. A variety of solutions are effective, and they depend on the resources you have at hand.

Here is a list of some strategies and resources:

- Talk to your professors immediately. They are happy to help you. They prefer it if you tell them you're having difficulty, rather than puzzling later when you don't do well; they are more inclined to be disappointed then. All faculty have office hours—use them. Speak to your professors after class to make an appointment; send an email or call. Explain honestly what you do not understand.

- Form study groups. Pulling together diverse mindsets can assure that collectively you can crack the code of whatever issues are in front of you. Each of you offers different strengths.

- Make use of the small group settings that may be offered along with large lecture classes, which do not lend themselves to discussion or questioning. The **recitation or discussion** sections (sometimes called seminars) are usually registered for at the same time as the class. They may be led by the instructor or by a graduate student (**teaching assistant, or TA**). This is where you're expected to raise questions. The goal is to ensure that everyone is on track. There is no stigma attached to inquiry—your questions may be the ones everyone else has too. You can also see the TA on your own.

- Take collective action if the problem is collective. It may come to light that many classmates are also in the dark about what is going on. Sometimes this is the fault of the professor, who could be lecturing over your heads (the professor who usually teaches graduate students and is assigned to teach a group of freshmen) or who may have issues organizing material. You can then agree as a group to raise the issues disturbing you to the professor, and designate a spokesperson. In dire cases—when you, as an entire class, feel that the instructor is not presenting the material in comprehensible ways, is frequently absent, or behaves in inappropriate ways—go as a group to the department chair to share your concerns.

- Go to the tutoring center, writing center, or learning center, often staffed by graduate students or upperclassmen, guided by professionals who are good at the skill or subject at hand. The staff get paid for this work, and it often supports their education too (a way you can help support other students). While these resources are for all students, they tend to be used most commonly not by struggling students but by better students trying to go from a B to an A grade. If they are not embarrassed to be seen there, you should not be either.
- Use workshops. Most campuses also have workshops on study and time management skills, which are usually sadly underattended or not attended at all by the students who really need the help offered. If you're really shy about it, find out who's running the workshop and plan to meet with them individually.

To repeat, if you're having difficulty, the main thing is to seek help. The resources, paid for by your tuition, are there.

What if it's only one class that is the problem? You're doing well in all the others because you love them, but there's that pesky math or language requirement. Here is another list of options:

- Tutoring (see above)
- Take a **placement test** to be sure you're in the correct class level. You may have scored high enough on your SAT or ACT, but the class you're placed in is being taught at a level above your skills. You can

ask to be tested to see if your skills match the school's standards for its courses. If they don't, you may be allowed to take a more appropriate-level class to allow you to build your skills and confidence.

- Check on your learning skills. If you're tested for and found to have a learning disability, then you may be eligible for special compensations for test taking or submitting papers, or whatever is the right accommodation for you. Some students get all the way to college only to discover that they had an issue all along that was not caught in a less rigorous environment. The **Americans with Disabilities Act (ADA)** requires that accommodations be offered for your needs.

- Take the class **pass/fail** if that is an option at your school for your situation. Pass/fail (sometimes called credit/no credit) means that if your work in the course is above a passing level (whatever that is for your school), you receive a grade of "pass," rather than the actual C or D you might have earned. Thus it will not affect your GPA negatively. On the other hand, if you fail, it will be noted as such, and you are not given credit for the class. In some cases, you cannot do pass/fail for your general education (required or core) course requirements or your major. Consult your school catalog to see if pass/fail is an option and how it works.

- Take the class again. Even if you struggle through the first time, your low grade can be superseded by a better one, even if the earlier one also shows on your transcript. Anyone later reading the transcript will see that you eventually learned the subject matter. Your school has rules about how this process is factored into your GPA and about how often it can be done.

- Drop the class (and try again later if necessary). You must take this action early in the term, within what some schools designate an add-drop period, when you can test out classes. Look at your college's **academic calendar** to find out the last day to drop without the class showing up on your transcript. After this date, the class is listed on your transcript, but with a W designation, indicating a withdrawal—but it does not affect your GPA. You don't want a slew of them on your transcript, however, as they may suggest to a potential employer or graduate program that you disappear in tough times. If you miss the early drop date, the last day to withdraw is usually shortly after midterms. Once that date has passed, you are out of luck.

Info: Drop Below Twelve Credits, Lose Financial Aid

You can lose your financial aid if you fall below full-time student status, which is typically twelve credits or more in a semester. This can happen easily by mistake. If you're taking twelve credits and become overwhelmed and decide to drop a class, then you've fallen below the limit. If you fail a course, that can put you below the limit. The government, which is handing out Pell grants or state aid, monitors students to see that they are making normal and satisfactory progress toward completion of the degree. When you fall below the mandated guidelines for yearly credits earned and attempted, then you risk losing your aid. You may then find that you're liable for the tuition expenses for that semester.

This is why it's so important to discuss challenging classes and strategies to deal with them. You must confer with someone who can help you think about the implications of your decisions and the choices you have. For example, you may be able to take a leave of absence or an Incomplete grade, rather than drop below the key threshold. Your advisor will be able to help you with this.

- Discuss the possibility of taking an **Incomplete** for the class. You must negotiate this with the instructor, who may let you submit the paper or other assignments in the next term. Rules vary by school, but generally you have only a few months or a semester to complete the work, or the **Inc** grade becomes an F.

- If you miss an exam or know that you won't be able to take it when scheduled (a trip for work, wife delivering a baby that day), talk to your professor and see about taking **a make-up exam**. Instructors don't like this arrangement because they have to make a special exam to avoid the possibility of cheating, which is extra work. Typically you are required to produce some evidence of why you missed or will miss an exam. Oversleeping doesn't usually satisfy the powers that be. A funeral, an illness, or a boss who won't give way are valid reasons and can be documented, although the request to do so may seem crass at the time. Some schools set special dates for make-ups, so that all are taken at one time.

- Take the course during the summer or at another time or school. Be sure to get approval beforehand. Because schools have differing levels of rigor, they usually want to be sure you're meeting the standards expected at your home campus. Some courses may have the same title, but somewhat different content. In that case, be prepared to show during the **pre-approval process** a sample of the syllabus or catalog course description from the school where you intend to enroll. This also holds true if you take time off and want to continue taking courses elsewhere, or make up for requirements or low grades you had from a bad experience.

A Cautionary Tale: Adin's Outside Courses

Adin was required, because of low first-year grades, to take a term off. During that time he chose to take some classes at an excellent local college, intending to apply the credits at his home campus when he returned there. He did not, however, get pre-approval to transfer the credits, and ultimately the situation interfered with his timely graduation. To complete his degree, he had to take the classes again, this time with the pre-approval.

> *Lessons learned:* Discuss any outside courses with your advisor or department, and get whatever approvals are needed early.

Another source of problems, on occasion, is a conflict with an instructor. Sometimes it's a matter of cultural or language differences, or even point of view. I recall an instance where a politically conservative professor taught a course on welfare systems at a large research university, where, with great regularity, he upset some portion of the class. Some students would drop the class, and some would seethe in silence; others protested to the dean, who had heard it all before.

Some students may cope with such situations by being rude or arrogant in class or in their dealings with instructors. This is not a good strategy, as it irritates the instructors and can lead to a negatively skewed perception that can even affect your grades. If a professor is genuinely offensive, however, speak to the department chair and also see how many other students have the same concern.

Misunderstandings between students and professors do occur sometimes. If the matter is more personal than pedagogical, go to a dean or **ombudsman** (a neutral arbitrator) for resolution of the dispute. Also know that all campuses, by federal law, have strict rules about **sexual harassment** and how such matters are to be handled. See your college's catalog, website, or counseling center for help—and do not delay. Persons trained to assist in these cases deal with sexual harassment in a fully confidential manner.

Info: Appeals and Petitions

There are some policies or practices of which students fall afoul so frequently that formal procedures and mechanisms exist to help resolve problems. Infractions or issues can range from blocked registration to late registration and problems with requirements to taking courses off campus. Such problems have significant consequences—they can prevent you from graduating on time or maintaining your full-time status. Find out if there are appeals or petitions processes on your campus. They may not be listed in the school catalog or on the website, and you may have to inquire at the registrar's or dean's offices or with your advisor, who may have the relevant forms and deadline information.

Before you give up or go ballistic out of frustration, be sure you've sought out this information. In clear-cut cases, for instance where you have hit the wrong key and wound up registering for the wrong course, thus missing the registration deadline, there can be a simple fix. It is important, in any case, that you are polite and provide evidence and any supporting documentation for your case, such as a note from an advisor or professor (on their letterhead).

Such processes, where they exist, are usually organized to be quickly responsive to the students' needs and the necessary timelines. You do not, however, always win your appeal, especially if you are clearly at fault or are a repeat offender making the same error. You can't claim you didn't know the registration process by your junior year, unless you are a transfer. A new review of your case is only likely when there is fresh and compelling information. And do not try to bully a new decision out of the appeals body. It may be made up of persons whose help you might need in other situations.

Finally, we repeat, do not go to the college president, who will only send the inquiry back to the review body that made the original decision.

You can **dispute a grade**, though it takes some work. Generally, you'll find a formal appeal process in the catalog or on the website. Typically, deadlines are set within a month or so for raising a dispute—you cannot wait six months to bring a case. The process generally begins with a conversation with your professor. Keep copies of any email triggering that conversation, as proof that you were within the deadlines.

If the meeting with your instructor does not go as you hope, then you may approach the department chair. There may be a body charged with hearing formal grade disputes where both student and instructor give evidence supporting their positions. You cannot just claim, though, that you worked hard and think you deserve a higher grade. The determination is made on evidence. It is likely the professor will bring evidence attempting to show you did not fulfill all the requirements for the course, paper, or exam involved. It's a good idea to talk to a dean or advisor before you begin a grade appeal process, to get a reality check or strategic guidance on how to best approach it.

Another manifestation of academic trouble for a student is landing on **probation**. This can happen when you don't heed the early warning signs that your grades are not in a passing range. Probation is a warning, and the next step is more serious and can mean suspension. Probation rules vary from school to school, but they generally are activated by a GPA below 2.0. You usually know you're in trouble before you get the official letter—you likely have been in denial, hiding under the bed for some time. Letting your grades reach this level is a real threat to your future. But the situation is not insoluble.

If you find yourself in a situation like this, it may be a clue that you're in the wrong courses. For example, about a third of all students who enter college intending to be premed and find that the required college-level science courses are much different from those in high school, and much harder or less engaging. This is a point where students frequently take a tumble. Instead, look at where you're doing well and regroup.

You must meet with an advisor and create an action plan for salvaging your college career. You likely will be permitted to stay, but you'll have to pull up your grades by a fixed time. Check with the financial aid office to determine the impact on your aid. Dropping below a certain GPA can threaten your scholarships, for instance. Use the earlier list of suggestions to pull up your grades. (This is also a good time to look at the first chapter of this book and also at the sections on choosing courses.)

If you do pull up your grades, probation will then be seen as a blip on your record and a learning experience from which you recovered. If your aid is affected to a degree that does not permit you to continue, take time off, work, and plan to come back. But do not quit—change your approach instead.

If you do not change, and you make the same mistakes again, you are likely to face **suspension**—a period of time in which you temporarily may not take classes. Again, this is not the end of the world (it may feel like it at the time, however). Take classes elsewhere (with pre-approval), and spend the time away in a job or service that shows you can be responsible. You may also be able to appeal a suspension, but you must have a compelling reason (medical evidence, a diagnosis of a learning disability or psychological issues, a major family crisis such as a parent's death). That you did not seek help before the bottom fell out will be challenged, however. By seeking help early, you also have advocates who can help in an appeal situation.

The worst case is **expulsion**—where you are removed from school permanently. This signifies that you have done something truly terrible. It may be a disciplinary infraction having to do with violence, weapons, drugs, alcohol, or sex. It may be repeated cheating or failure. In any event, there is normally a judiciary process where you're able to defend your position, if it is defensible. You may have an advocate to support you. If you have caused someone bodily harm or are caught with a weapon on campus, there is little recourse. Such situations can even lead to criminal prosecution, given the circumstances.

Expulsion for academic reasons means that you have generally had several warnings and opportunities to change and have not done so. There may be underlying issues of self-destruction that could require counseling or other support, but the institution has determined that you cannot successfully remain, and they are no longer willing to invest resources in you.

After time passes and you show evidence of real change, you may be able to seek readmittance. It is usually better to try a different college, though. An expulsion on your record does make it more difficult to enroll elsewhere, but again, time off spent well may help as evidence of reform.

In a state of panic, some students resort to the really unintelligent step of cheating or plagiarizing. As we've said before, academic integrity is taken extremely seriously. Some schools have **honor systems**, wherein students self-police and are supported in reporting one another's transgressions of the rules. Professors also have new tools to identify where students have cheated or plagiarized. Anyone caught cheating or plagiarizing faces serious consequences.

Usually a judicial process exists on campus to deal with such matters. You are expected to prove that you did not violate school rules. Your professor also amasses evidence to prove that you did violate them, and a dean or a body made up of deans, faculty, and even students may hear the case. If it's proven that you've transgressed, it is *not* a good thing to have on your record, and the penalties range from failing the paper or exam to failing the class, being suspended, or even expelled (usually for flagrant or repeated infractions).

A Cautionary Tale: Cole's Third Strike

Cole was from a wealthy and powerful family, which he thought would protect him from ever having to pay the consequences for his actions. A week before graduation, he was brought up on charges for plagiarizing. When the dean's review committee noted that he had a third case before them (the previous ones involved late papers and cheating), he was suspended. All of these charges would appear on his permanent record and would follow him on his career path.

<u>Lesson learned:</u> *Do not cut corners and try to get away with bad behavior. Don't think your family, money, threats, or even a previously good record erase its impact.*

There are far too many stories to tell of students who have allowed panic or arrogance to cloud their judgment and have destroyed promising college careers. *Get help and support early.* You can reach out to individuals both at school and among wise adults you know from family, work, or a religious institution. Talk to the ones you trust and who care about your future.

HEALTH AND WELL-BEING CRISES

There is an expression in Latin, *mens sana in corpore sano*, which means "a sound mind in a sound body." You cannot do well in college (or in life) without taking care of your physical and mental well-being. Among the advantages of college life are the free health facilities for students (covered by your tuition and fees), gym facilities, and counseling services, as well as the major medical care that may be covered by your parents or family, insurance from an employer, or by low-cost policies that you're mandated to take out on entry to college if you have no other coverage. You may be covered by Medicaid if you qualify; if you move out of state, you should check your eligibility in the state where you're going. This type of information is in the materials you get when you're accepted. You can also find it on the college website, or discuss it with college officials. If you're not taking the school's health insurance policy, but are covered by another program, a formal waiver form is included.

Although as a young person (or one young in spirit) you may not feel vulnerable, you should take advantage of these resources. The health center offers free or low-cost flu shots, for example, as well as medications for minor ailments like colds and cramps. For major concerns, the center generally maintains a relationship or an affiliation with a local hospital, unless your school itself has a teaching hospital on campus as part of its medical school. When you start to feel unwell, it is best to quickly visit the health facility or your doctor. You are now part of a wider community, and it is easy to communicate diseases to others.

There are many common illnesses on college campuses. The best-known disease among college students is mononucleosis (often called the kissing disease), which causes you to be extremely tired, among other symptoms. Meningitis is another highly communicable disease on campuses requiring all who have been in contact with the affected student to be tested and treated. Sexually transmitted diseases (STDs) and AIDS are also major concerns. The health center deals as much with prevention as with treatment, and may provide courses on how to prevent STDs or other afflictions. You are also required to submit evidence that you have had measles shots before you even enter college. While measles and mumps are both rare among adults, they are highly contagious and can have very serious consequences, including sterility for men. At the first sign of symptoms, it is important to see a medical provider, to be sure you don't have something serious and transmittable.

Be sure to have any necessary medications with you, and keep your prescriptions on file at the school health facility or a local drug store. (Note that abusing your drugs, or worse, selling them to others, can lead to dismissal or prosecution or both.) Wear a bracelet indicating any allergies. Keep a physician-prescribed EpiPen® on hand in case you're subject to severe allergic reactions. If you have a chronic illness, alert the school, so they can be sure to help you and have a plan in case of emergencies.

Disabilities are not barriers to success. Check in with the office that deals with ADA (Americans with Disabilities Act) issues and compliance. For disabilities that are inherent, such as deafness, blindness, or a physical infirmity, wheelchair ramps, signing, or seeing-eye dogs are all means of coping that are available on campus. And even if your disability is temporary—a football injury or a sprain from a tumble on an icy sidewalk—the school must still provide support and accommodations.

A Story: Isabel

Isabel was a returning student who had lost her sight as an adult. She had managed to raise a family, but was a single mother and had to go back to school to increase her earning ability. She navigated around her campus with a cane, and the college provided special computers that gave her access to her work in Braille or sound. Isabel graduated at the top of her class and is now earning a doctorate in physics.

If you're sick, be sure to tell a dean or advisor who can let all your professors know that you will be away from classes. They may ask for a doctor's note if you have not seen the health center on campus. Even if you're in the campus infirmary or home in bed and well enough, you may be able to keep up with work online. I have taken books and assignments to students in the infirmary, and even once took an exam there myself.

The gym or **athletic facilities** are a huge resource, where you can get the benefits of the best health club at no cost. You can take classes in yoga or African dance, or join **intramural teams** (playing among students on your campus only). You may discover a sport you had never considered, like lacrosse, track, or tennis. At the same time, the gym can give you the release you need in times of stress. You can work out in a weight room, or hit a punching bag, or jog around a track to release tension, think, or just clear your head and loosen joints cramped from sitting long hours at a computer.

Obviously, if you've been recruited for a varsity sport, the gym is your second home, the coach is like a parent, and your teammates become your second family. Keep balance in mind, however, as you don't want your sport to take so much of your time that your schoolwork suffers. All it takes is one injury to derail an athletic career, and you need your academic record to sustain your plans for future success.

There are plenty of exercise opportunities outside the gym as well. Even some urban campuses have tree-lined spaces where you can go to work out or run, surrounded by plants and flowers. If you are lucky enough to be on the coast (east or west), you might have a beach on or near campus. Evidence shows that a good workout, even for a half-hour a day, can go a long way toward both physical and mental well-being.

PERSONAL/EMOTIONAL CRISES

Challenges in your personal life can result in emotional stress and distress. These stresses are sometimes difficult to confront because they make you feel out of place or incapable of coping, which can feel demeaning. So we often deny the pain we're feeling, and then it pops up in a new form—sadness over a breakup can pop up as overeating, stress about a family matter may lead to drinking too much, concern about appearance can show up as exercising to excess or binge eating.

You may have stress due to physical issues or a neurobehavioral issue, such as attention deficit disorder (ADD), addictive behavior, or depression. If so, know that you are not alone. Sixty-seven percent of students with depression or anxiety do not report it or ask for help—don't let that be you.

Social-worker-turned-successful-entrepreneur Terrie Williams writes of her own depression and that of many well-known figures in her book *Black Pain*. She notes that persons of color or from cultures outside the United States are more inclined to suppress personal issues, which does not serve us well in the long term. I have known students who wanted therapy, but feared that if their parents found out, it would be taken as a sign of weakness, or there would be concern that family dirty laundry was being aired among strangers. Don't succumb to these fears; help is there for you; seek it out.

Campuses offer facilities and resources to deal with these issues, and some report that their counselors and professional staff have seen as much as half of the student body. It's a sign of your desire to survive and thrive that you seek help.

Campus resources can range from full medical teams to psychiatrists or social workers, all trained to deal with various kinds of physical, psychological, and emotional issues, both short- and long-term. Some resources may be able to offer medication and others therapy; some may be able to do both. Some schools have ties to other schools or medical facilities where even more extensive resources are provided.

For help that is both free and anonymous, on or near campus there are usually AA meetings or other twelve-step programs such as Nicotine Anonymous, ACOA (Adult Children of Alcoholics), NA (Narcotics Anonymous), OA (Overeaters Anonymous), Debtors Anonymous, or Al-anon, for those with families or friends with addiction issues. You can access any of these support systems by contacting your advisor, RA, dean, chaplain, or even a trusted professor. You can find AA and other programs in the telephone book or through a search engine. Getting help is a good thing. In fact, sometimes it may be best to even interrupt your college career with a **leave of absence**, to take time away and regroup with the help of appropriate professionals.

Depression is now accepted as a real health issue with physical as well as psychological components and manifestations. We speak of being depressed when we are sad or down. But often we are walking around in a depressed state without knowing what it is. Causes can be bio-physical or situational. Some circumstances in college can trigger situational depression: homesickness, missing old friends, not making new friends fast enough, having too much work to do, having concerns about money, feeling alone in your confusion, starting a new relationship or ending an old one, and worrying about your family. It is not uncommon to be dealing with several of these at one time, when any one can be a bear all by itself.

If you feel overwhelmed, want to do nothing but sleep, avoid others, abuse drugs or alcohol, eat nothing or too much, or cry at the drop of a hat, then you may be suffering from depression.

A Story: Asako

Asako was a beautiful young woman from a stable family. She was doing well in school until her senior year. She had gained a little weight, but not enough to be troubling, and in fact, she may have needed the additional pounds. During the holidays, like most of us, she gained a bit more, but she then began to berate herself. When she came back to campus, she began bingeing and purging and became ill and lethargic. This condition kept her away from her classes, and she fell behind in her work, which then added to her feelings of guilt and failure. Asako's situation snowballed into depression, and soon she was emotionally paralyzed and her health was in jeopardy. She was encouraged to take some time off and to see a therapist. Her work with the therapist had her back in school in a few months with a new outlook and skills for dealing with her self-perception.

Seeking help is better than self-medicating. One of the biggest problems on campuses these days is the use and abuse of prescription drugs to manage mood and productivity. The risk is high for addiction and permanent damage to both physical and mental health. Rather than delve here into the issues raised by campus use of various drugs, I suggest you go to the site **http://www.drugabuse.gov/students-young-adults**, which breaks down the facts by drug.

While headlines report student deaths, they seldom report the cases of long-term damage from drug use, in which abusers permanently harm themselves, and in many cases harm others. You are at an age when you feel nothing can go wrong, but the statistics show that belief is a fallacy. Most teens arrested test positive for drugs or alcohol, which speaks to another risk to your reputation and ultimate employability. Sale and abuse of drugs can show up on your college record and also lead to expulsion or suspension from school. Another side effect is that drugs make you unattractive. (Google "drug abuse pictures" and see the YouTube before-and-afters—then decide if that's where you want to go.) The "benefits" as perceived in the moment are fleeting, the risks lasting and not worth it. A good film on the topic is *Requiem for a Dream*, starring Jennifer Connelly, which reveals the gritty, dark side of substance abuse. You do not want to find yourself there.

On the other hand, the issue may not be your problem, but that of someone close to you. Your friend is acting weird, or smells of beer all the time, or is threatening suicide. How can you intervene? Can you even intervene? One student came to me for an extension on a paper with the reason that she was distracted by a roommate who kept trying to commit suicide. Clearly, she was looking for a way to get help for her roommate without seeming to "rat" on her.

It's better to reveal a problem or concern than to feel the guilt if something does go very wrong. It is often those who see a student on a regular basis who can pick up on the need for help. Professors have called me when a student is weepy in class or too angry or just absent a lot. Sometimes a peer advisor or RA, trained in how to respond, notices what is going on. Or it may be you who notices. If so, you can offer to go with a friend to a counseling center or a twelve-step meeting. You should tell someone if there is a real risk to yourself or others in the long-term or in the moment as a result of a friend's behavior. (Certainly you know not to let friends drink and drive.) A counselor can help you plan an intervention if needed. The main thing is not to keep your well-founded concerns to yourself.

Campus Resources

Every campus has resources available to help during crises, although they may vary depending on the campus. What resources might you find on campus?

College Infirmary or Health Center

- Here the staff includes full- or part-time doctors and nurses who can diagnose and often treat a range of illnesses. For highly contagious diseases or complex matters, the center partners with local hospitals and medical facilities with full capacity to deal with all major health problems. The health center can usually dispense over-the-counter and some prescription drugs, and provide bed rest for severe colds or flu, when a student should be away from the main school population. On a commuter campus, the center may send you home.
- Services are free or at minimal cost. The centers can provide immunizations, as well as tests for HIV and other diseases; they can even give shots for travel abroad. A source of health and wellness education, they often have students on staff who are trained to help inform the college population about how to keep healthy.
- When you find it necessary to request an extension or an Incomplete

from an instructor, the health center can provide verification that you have been unwell and seen by a medical professional. (Whenever you need to let a professor know that you've been absent due to illness, get a note on letterhead from your doctor.)

Counseling Center

- This is where you find trained professionals who deal with mental health issues such as anxiety attacks, depression, or addictive behaviors. They may be psychiatrists or social workers trained in clinical psychology, and they can provide therapeutic services on a short- or long-term basis. The number of visits you can make to the campus-based counselors varies from school to school. For long-term needs, a list of approved providers is available, usually indicating low cost. Often you can get referrals to providers who offer sliding-scale fee arrangements or take insurance, so that the cost is not so prohibitive you cannot afford the help you need.

- Know that therapy takes time and is not a one-shot fix. On the other hand, there may be times when you need a counselor to help you deal in the short term with an immediate situation, such as the death of a family member or a divorce.

- The benefits and skills you acquire from being in counseling are lifelong. *These services are completely confidential, and not even other administrators or family members have access to what occurs in these sessions, unless you give permission in person or in writing.*

Peer Advisors or Residence Hall Advisors

- These are students trained to interact with other students regarding personal issues, in particular the adjustment to college. Sometimes it is easier to start a conversation with someone your own age. The peer advisor or RA may determine that other resources or persons on campus might be helpful, but they are a good starting place for practical advice and sometimes just a reality check. Another student can let you know that what you're feeling may be quite common stress or insecurity, which many students experience.

Deans

- Though you would see an academic dean for issues relating to your schoolwork (and other issues as well, depending on your relationship), there are also deans whose job it is to focus on various aspects of student life on campus. They usually have titles such as Dean of Students or Student Affairs or Student Life.
- Go to these deans regarding any issues related to these areas. They enjoy students and want to see that you have a good experience, so they want to hear what your concerns or issues are. At the same time, they are responsible for the well-being and safety of all students and enforce the rules fairly, but firmly. They are generally the deans who deal with matters of non-academic discipline, such as drunkenness or sexual harassment.

Chaplains

- Sometimes you're more comfortable bringing your concerns to someone from a faith community. Like the counseling center, chaplains hold confidences. They may take the place of your home parish priest, minister, rabbi, or imam. They may provide comfort and solace using their own faith practice and skills, and they may also suggest you use additional campus or other resources as needed.

Ombudsman

- Conflicts can occur that seem to be more personal than academic or that don't seem to fit under normal disciplinary channels—bias or just bad chemistry, for instance. These can be disputes between or among students and faculty, students and other students, or students and administrators. It's clear that the usual rules won't help and that someone needs to be an objective outsider to mediate the conflict.

- Not every campus has an ombudsman's office, but where it does exist, it can be quite useful in bringing down the temperature of all concerned and hammering out a resolution that may not be ideal for all sides, but will be fair.

Professors

- Your faculty can be wonderful allies in times of stress. If you have made a positive impression on one or more professors, then they want to help you get through tough times. They can certainly give you extra time to get work done if there is a real crisis, and they may offer a receptive ear over a cup of coffee (not a beer).
- Professors must observe limits and boundaries, as they must be fair to all of their students. They should not overstep proprieties by becoming too personally involved with any one student. But they were once students themselves or have known others in your circumstances and can offer a friendly perspective. Like the peer advisor, they may guide you to other resources and may ask your permission to share your problem with a dean or others who can help.

Athletic Facility

- For some student-athletes, the coach is their most trusted person and advocate. As with faculty members, coaches must observe barriers in terms of appropriate behavior, but they are certainly invested in your success, and you can seek them out in a time of crisis.
- Using the athletic facilities can be helpful—working out in some way can be a great way to deal with stress. The coach or fitness trainer is also trained to deal with troubled students and may even spot problems manifested as lack of stamina, missed practices, or too much weight loss.

Remember FERPA, the privacy act—no one on campus can reveal to anyone who is not an administrator anything about your life without your permission. Clergypersons, doctors, and therapists can't even reveal your confidences to administrators without your permission. Your risk in sharing with someone is very limited, and the benefits are great.

The worst thing you can do is hold in whatever is troubling you and delay in getting some guidance. Sometimes the solution is easier than you can imagine, and by delaying you only add to the burden by becoming more and more immersed in fear that intensifies.

A Cautionary Tale: Anita Overdoes It

As a result of bad planning, Anita had worked overtime on final papers, staying up days at a time on coffee and amphetamines. By the time her papers were done, she was physically worn out, but she still had to help run a campus event that involved lots of running around campus in the snow. The combination of drugs, no sleep, and stress led to her skipping a period, and she feared she was pregnant. She did not tell anyone, though.

She came down with bronchitis, and her friends became worried. She was so sick and depressed she would not leave her room. One of them called Anita's mother, who came to campus and took her home. On the way Anita tearfully revealed the feared pregnancy to her mom. As soon as she got home and the burden of the secret was revealed, however, her period returned.

She had to deal with the implications of the situation with her parents, which was not easy. It took a couple of weeks for Anita to get better. She lost time at school, but all was ultimately well.

Lesson learned: Overdoing and self-medicating can have a snowball effect, with both physical and psychological implications.

OTHER KINDS OF CRISES

Besides academic and health or personal crises, you may encounter financial ones, or challenges associated with jobs or family responsibilities. The same rule applies: talk to someone.

In the case of fear of **loss of financial aid or tuition funds**, go first to the financial aid office. *Be sure you fill out the FAFSA form whenever it's due, so that even if you are the rare student who does not get or need aid, you are in the system in case of an emergency.* If your tuition was covered by an employer and you lose the job or they cut that benefit, go to the financial aid office at once. There may be adjustments that the office can make, or scholarships or loans that it can make available. Some schools have **revolving loan funds** in case a student is the victim of theft, fire, or a temporary crisis. (You must file a police or security report in these situations.) Try in every way not to drop out of school, as you would be deferring potentially higher income for longer. Taking a larger student loan is the better investment in the long term.

In crises that occur in families—illness, death, divorce, and even incarceration of family members—you need to make these first priority. Let a school official know (by email preferably, for the purpose of documentation) that you're dealing with a personal matter. Share as much as you can comfortably. The dean, advisor, or chaplain will be happy to contact professors to let them know you need time away, will miss some classes, or may need a make-up exam. I knew one student who was so focused on school and so in shock that she showed up for an early appointment one day, even though her mother had died overnight. I sent her home and contacted her professors for her.

A Story: Benjamin

Benjamin was from a successful family and had never had problems with school. During the winter break his grandmother, to whom he was devoted, died suddenly. He had planned to write papers over the break, but he was overwhelmed with sorrow as well as with funeral arrangements and his parents' grief. Benjamin could not do his schoolwork.

After break he went to his dean to ask for an extension and apologized repeatedly for his "failure" to get the work done. The dean explained that the extension was meant for such a circumstance (as opposed to the student with a hangover) and that there was no reason to feel he had failed in any way. With the burden lifted, Benjamin got the work done a few weeks late, but done. He also sought out grief counseling through the counseling center, so that he could deal with his feelings and figure out how best to support his parents too.

Family pressures can create stress and crisis. It is not unusual for young people to take on more than they should—caring for younger brothers and sisters, or feeling their parents have sacrificed for them and that they are obligated to do whatever they're told in compensation. Again, the idea is balance and focus. If you complete school, you are in a better place to support your family. So there are times when you need to say no and move your education and future up higher in your list of priorities.

Counselors can help you see where your responsibilities appropriately begin and end, and how to balance them. If you can shop for an elderly neighbor who can, in turn, look in on a younger sibling, do so. Take a job that fits your career goals, and bring home some of your pay, instead of working in the family business, which may not build your résumé. If you have young children, some schools have **day-care programs** that can take family burdens off, for instance. Be creative, but protect your future. Administrators have seen all of this before and can offer ideas and resources.

In some cases—when, for example, you have a chance to travel abroad or for a research opportunity—your family may resist just as you are making your plans. A dean or an advisor can help them see how the opportunity helps you in the long run, and how much prestige it brings to you and the whole family. It's a good idea, if you are honored at any time, to bring along a family member to bask in your glory. They are usually more supportive as a result.

Relationships can be an enormous source of stress, as discussed earlier. If extremely challenging scenarios exist, such as an abusive relationship or pregnancy, colleges are prepared to work with you. For a pregnancy, they may grant you a leave of absence, allow you to do some work from home, or give you Incompletes. Schools have even worked with young fathers who were trying to figure out how to stay in school and also be supportive of a new, if unplanned, family.

If there is abuse in a relationship, then you should bring both **campus security** and counseling services into the picture. If the abuser is a student, the college institutes disciplinary proceedings. If it is someone from outside your college community, the college can put in place restraining orders or prohibit the abuser from appearing on campus, in cooperation with local authorities.

We include **date rape** here as a form of horrific abuse. Date rape is defined as unwanted sexual relations between two individuals who know each other and have some form of relationship. It is often facilitated by drugs, called "date rape" drugs, which are put in a drink and knock you out. (Learn more at **www.womenshealth.gov**.) Just drinking too much can also put you at risk. The resulting devastation is increased because one partner has breached the presumed trust of the other.

Like any assault, date rape should be reported. With that being said, we must acknowledge that young men have been falsely accused out of spite or misguided thinking; this is also criminal and can destroy lives. No accusation of assault should be taken lightly on either side. It is crucial to speak to someone immediately to get the help you need, including hospital attention. Colleges want to retain you and protect you. Be sure to get the help you need.

Info: Campus Security

Campus Security is your friend. They can protect you when you're out on campus late, come to your aid in a crisis, open your dorm room when you've left your key inside, keep the unwanted from your door, and get you to the hospital in an emergency. Know the campus security number. Given recent violent events on some campuses, now there are often alert systems that you should be plugged into. Alerts can concern events as benign as snowstorm warnings or as urgent as word of an attack on campus.

In some instances, you may have **legal issues** relating to circumstances such as divorce, housing disputes, or employment discrimination. If your college has an affiliated law school, you may use a legal clinic that serves students. Some schools have arrangements with local legal agencies or law firms offering pro bono (free) services. Your local government may offer resources, to which the college can connect you. If you have **immigration issues**, you typically can find an office that deals with international students. The dean of students is most likely to know of such resources.

COLLEGE IS FOR LEARNING LIFE SKILLS

College is a place where you transition from one level of knowledge, self-awareness, and maturity to another. Given that reality, colleges are prepared to help you deal with the challenges that come with these transitions. The skills you learn now that get you through crises are tools you draw on for years to come—the "real" world, or life after college, can be much less forgiving and far less supportive. Thus, employers value the person who can 'fess up to mistakes and learn from them. Families do better when members know how to seek out resources as needed. The important thing to know is that this is the best place to seek help and support, because it is, perhaps, the most forgiving environment you'll ever encounter.

Chapter 10
PREPARING FOR LIFE AFTER COLLEGE

While you're in college, you're always preparing for what comes next. It is difficult, though, to actually make that next move to leave—you've gotten pretty comfortable with life in school. Leaving what has become familiar is always scary. I remember a commencement speaker saying to a graduating class that they had climbed this ladder to the pinnacle of success, had gotten their degrees, and now they were getting ready to step off that ladder—into nothing! What a disheartening message! You don't have to step off into nothing. Just keep in mind, the word "commencement" means "beginning," even though it celebrates the end of this phase of your schooling and your life. Along the way, you can put in place the structure you'll step onto next.

Remember the discussion about choosing a major. You've been building skill sets to serve you in your next phase. You should be a much better writer now. You should know how to do research. You should know how to think critically and support contentions with evidence. You now have facts and information you never dreamed you would. You are more interesting and able to converse and relate to more people. As you learned to overcome obstacles and use the resources at hand, you established practices and behaviors that will serve you well in your new life. And you will be surprised, along life's path, at how randomly things crop up that you remember and find useful. When I'm reading newspapers, or even mystery novels, and find references to "great books" of literature, I smile as I remember reading them when I was a college student.

Perhaps most important, you built a support network of classmates and even faculty and administrators who can continue to be there for you for years to come. The best man at your wedding, the godparents for your children, the person writing letters of reference for your jobs, perhaps your spouse or business partner, likely may come from the ranks of those individuals you met in college. These ties hold ("the old school tie"), even more than those from high school or your neighborhood. You shared experiences, stresses, and successes. My college class has a Google group where we keep up with one another pretty regularly, even after forty years. Always remember your network when you are working through the issues right after school.

What are the biggest issues after college? First is deciding what you're going to do next. It may be work, or it may be graduate or professional school. We suggested that you begin working toward these goals early on. Now let's delve more deeply into exactly what you need to do to be prepared for and accepted in whatever you plan as your next step. Remember, you should have a plan A and a plan B, given contractions in doctoral program admissions, graduate school funding, and the job market. Good preparation, however, goes a long way toward putting you at the top of the list.

Let's take a look first at preparing for graduate or professional school.

THE GRADUATE/PROFESSIONAL SCHOOL PLAN

A Story: Kalina

Kalina focused on predentistry while in college, but loved the literature classes she took for fun. When she graduated, she realized that she never really wanted to be a dentist—that was her father's dream. She wanted to be around words, so she worked in publishing for a long time. She did become restless, though, and decided to try her hand at finance, if only so she could understand that universe. Her work in publishing and finance led her to work in advocacy and communications relating to her family's native Ghana. Soon she was based on the African continent, engaged in life-saving work in a few war-torn countries. This type of high-stress work led to exhaustion, however, and proved a risk to her own life, so she returned home to rest for a while and grow her own family. Asked to help a local school, Kalina soon found herself as its head. Once she got the school on its feet again, she felt pulled to return to work on international affairs. She does not know what's next, but she does know that every one of her experiences has had value and that she has learned from each.

Applying to graduate or professional school is a job in itself, and you do it while you're fully engaged in the work of your senior year, finishing a thesis or research project, filling those final requirements, and spending time with friends you may not see again for a long time. So a plan of action is crucial.

A Checklist
Here are some key milestones for your graduate school application process.

Early Junior Year
☐ Begin test prep for whichever tests you are taking (GRE, GMAT, MCAT, LSAT). Buy the books, take the prep classes offered on or off campus, and do self-tests. Plan to take the test at the end of your junior year, so if you have to retake it, you have time to prepare over the coming summer and meet the schools' deadlines. *Do not assume you will score high the first time.*

Junior Year
☐ Meet with the advisor who guides students for graduate program or professional school admissions. There you can get help selecting the

right array of schools to apply to. For example, a good prelaw advisor knows the GPA and LSAT combinations necessary for acceptance into different tiers of schools. The premed advisor has the information for medical schools.

☐ Begin to budget for your applications and set aside money. Fees can add up to several hundreds of dollars. See if you qualify for **fee waivers** if you meet certain income guidelines. You may also want to plan for travel to visit schools. In some cases, schools interested in you may pay for your visit, but many do not. You may know or be able to find friends or school alumni on campuses of interest who are happy to host you for a visit. If you can get a firsthand feel for a campus, the programs, students, and culture of a place, you can make better choices about where you want to go. The ideal strategy is to have a summer research experience on a campus you're interested in, during the summer between junior and senior years.

End of Junior Year

☐ Research schools of interest. Talk to your faculty to learn about faculty in your field at other schools. Read articles by them or study their research. You may, in the case of doctoral programs, and if your work is closely aligned, want to contact them to express interest in working with them. In the case of professional schools, find out how alumni from your school are doing there and how their graduates are doing securing jobs.

☐ Line up all the professors you need to do recommendations for you. It could happen that the important professor you had counted on will be on sabbatical in the fall, or doing research in Latin America. Or a key professor may be lured away to another school. Get references from faculty who are full-time, not adjunct or part-time, unless they're prestigious in their own right, such as a former senator or mayor. Ideally, you've already had conversations with persons in your field of interest who can help you select schools or refer you to colleagues at the schools you're exploring.

Summer Before Senior Year

☐ Work on your personal statements. Share drafts with advisors or faculty. Expect to do several drafts. It is much easier to do them during the summer than in the fall, when you are taking classes and submitting applications.

☐ Request applications for all the schools you're considering, or download applications from the Web. Review their requirements and deadlines to determine what documents and information you need. For example, you need **transcripts**, which will come from your registrar. Sometimes you can get them within days, and sometimes it can take weeks. You may need to mail them directly to the schools, or you may include them (sealed in official envelopes) with your application package. Some schools charge fees for transcripts. Others provide the first few free and charge for more than three or four (another budget item!).

Early Fall of Senior Year

☐ Do a timeline for yourself, based on the due dates of the various applications. Note when you should have the personal statement done, recommendations in, transcripts on hand, and applications submitted or postmarked.

Fall of Senior Year

☐ Meet again with your advisors and faculty to refine your plans. By now you have taken any relevant tests at least once and know your standing and your GPA from junior year. Your final application list should include a stretch school or two, a safe school, and a few in between. The research you've done should reveal that several schools may have what you're looking for in terms of academic focus, faculty, climate, and school culture. Some are more appealing than others, but the ones you apply to should all feel like places where you could be happy and accomplish your goals. In some ways this process is similar to selecting undergraduate colleges to apply to, but in this case faculty ties and relationships are much more important. The stretch school requires a GPA and test scores a bit above where you are, but you should apply to at least one such school. You are well above the basic standard and fit just about all criteria of the safe school. The in-between schools are just that—you fairly closely fit the criteria. Do not plan to apply to more than ten schools—but ten is a good number to give yourself the best odds.

Pay Attention!

- ☐ Proofread, proofread, proofread—be sure there are no errors in your application, that you have not confused addresses of schools, and so forth. It is really easy to make and miss errors in an online application, so print out the elements and read them or ask others to do so too. Build in time for this review.

- ☐ Prepare for interviews. Not every school or program requires them, but many do. You must do your homework about the school or program you're applying to and the faculty with whom you may work. Reading about the department, articles by key professors, and journals in your field are good preparation. You also need to become comfortable engaging in discussion, however, and that requires practice. Ask your professors to put you through a mock graduate school interview—these are not the same as a job interview; you are revealing your scholarly knowledge. As with any interview, though, you must present yourself as likeable and friendly. No one wants to work with a curmudgeon.

- ☐ Breathe deeply and let it go. The worst aspect of applying to graduate or professional schools is the waiting. It may take months. Schools have varying application-acceptance cycles and processes, and these may be different even from department to department and discipline to discipline. Students hear as late as early May from some schools. When some of your classmates are hearing in March, it can be nerve-wracking. Do not despair, and do not haunt the admissions offices of your chosen schools. That just annoys them. Keep your plan B in mind, and say prayers for the best outcome. (If you're invited for an interview, it is a good sign.) Similar to when you applied to college, the stretch choice, though perhaps prestigious, may not be right for you.

A Story: Don

Don was a brilliant English literature major who knew by his junior year that he wanted to be a professor and would be applying to doctoral programs. He won every related award given to a graduating senior and was accepted by the PhD program at a prestigious Ivy League university. He was also accepted to a smaller state university. When he visited the two schools, he found that the Ivy campus did not have the faculty he would need to support his research. Even the Ivy agreed that for his work the state university was a better choice.

A Story: Althea

The brilliant Althea was part of a campus research program. She had an excellent GPA. Her interests were a bit eclectic, however. While her classmates had all heard from graduate schools and knew where they were going, she got letter after letter of rejection from some of the country's best schools. She was having serious doubts about herself, but then in May, at her low point, she was accepted to a state university that offered a program encompassing perfectly all her areas of interest. The program would be small and nurturing for her doctoral studies.

Info: Postgraduate Fellowships

As mentioned earlier, there are a host of fellowships for graduating seniors that carry great prestige and that, far from derailing your plans, can very much enhance them because of their prestige and competitive nature. Indeed, graduate and professional schools will happily defer your entrance if you win a Rhodes, Marshall, or Fulbright Fellowship—all of which take you abroad for a year or two. Postgraduate fellowships are funds that have been designated by their donors to support graduate study, enable internships or service, or facilitate postgraduate study abroad. While many of these awards are well known, some, like the National Science Foundation, Soros, or Ford, are generous but specialized. Some relate to specific fields, such as the Truman for public service or the James Madison for teaching American history. Some are government sponsored, coming from agencies such as NASA or the Department of Defense.

In every case, winning one is a signal mark of achievement that can open many doors. If you have a high GPA of 3.8 or above, and a record of service and general excellence, you really should consider applying for these and should seek support from your college in the application process.

These fellowships are transformative. Even the process of applying demands a level of self-searching that applicants say is of benefit in its own right. You really have to be able to articulate your path and your passion. These fellowships are investing in future leaders, so their expectations are highly rigorous for outstanding personal statements, references, and in some cases, interviews. If you are in the very top at your school, then go for it. The journey will be worth it.

A Story: Ryann

Ryann won a postgraduate fellowship that enabled her to engage in service in South Africa. She had planned to do a project on education and AIDS, but once there found that the issues were quite different from what she had envisioned and that she had to rethink her action plan. Today she is running a health-care collective in Sierra Leone. The fellowship changed her life path.

A Story: Mrs. Joy Moore

Mrs. Moore, a Black single mother with two amazing children, insisted on high standards, and both children attended prestigious colleges. Upon graduation, her son was named a Rhodes Scholar, and her daughter won a Jack Kent Cooke fellowship, which paid for two graduate degrees.

THE JOB SEARCH PLAN

Keeping your eye on the idea of work after graduation can help get you through college. But you need to remember that what you are seeking is your first job, not your last. Remember the Pauli Murray story. The reality is that for the first eight to ten years after graduation it is not uncommon to move around to as many as four different jobs. You'll be at the first rung of the career ladder.

Ideally you had internships that led you to make good choices about the kinds of jobs you want first, or they even led to job offers, but you're still trying out the work world. An internship lasts for a short time, and that colors the experience. You most likely don't have the same level of responsibility or pressure that you do if you're full-time. You always know during an internship that there is an exit strategy. When you exit a "real" job, it is for a better one, or because you were unsuccessful or got laid off. Your pay covers your real-life expenses, and so the pressure is more intense than in summer jobs or internships.

Under these conditions of greater pressure you can more realistically gauge if the field or the employer is right for you. You can decide that you love the field, but hate the employer, or hate the field, even though you love the employer. Perhaps it is not what you anticipated or your skills are not being put to the best use. You're in over your head, or the environment doesn't serve you well.

There are a number of different ways a company's environment may not suit you. One woman who did not drink found herself in an office that had a cocktail hour every day at 4 p.m., which made her really uncomfortable. Sadly, there are still workplaces where women are not treated with respect, or persons of color feel marginalized. Or you may end up falling in love with someone in another state. Some workplaces are more attuned to work-family balance than others.

At this stage of your life, expect to move around in your professional life as you find your footing and the right fit for all aspects of your intellectual and personal life. Making changes is not necessarily a sign of failure, and may be a sign of self-awareness. As you move on, however, be able to cite acceptable rationales for each move that future employers can understand.

But before you even get to tackle these challenges, you must land that first job. As with applying to graduate schools, your search for that first job also needs a plan of action. Some parts of that process help you develop skills that you'll use repeatedly. Remember, the free resources of the career office cost thousands later in life—like the gym, it is a "free" resource that your tuition actually pays for. You are fully entitled to use it to the maximum, and many schools let you continue to do so as an alumnus for the rest of your life. Following is a job search timeline that you can use in conjunction with those resources.

A Checklist

The Career Office

☐ Visit the career office and learn the resources that you can tap. Ideally, start doing this as a freshman or sophomore, You give yourself time to build your résumé that way. But any time up to the middle of your senior year is useful. By the second half of your senior year, it is late to start the process—not hopeless, but not *nearly* as effective.

☐ The office may offer tests that help you see your strengths and how they align with your interests or with fields you want to explore.

☐ Use the library of books on various career paths and what is expected. **Trade publications** are magazines that cater to particular fields—*Ad Age* for the advertising industry, *Women's Wear Daily* for the fashion and retail trade, for instance. These can reveal trends in the business, who is moving around, which firms are strong, and which are faltering. They can help you target your search and be more knowledgeable for your interviews. There are also online resources and blogs for particular industries.

☐ Watch for special presentations on campus by alumni or others in your field of interest. They can offer valuable information on what it's like to be in those fields and provide opportunities to network.

☐ See if there is an alumni network or mentor program that facilitates networking and **informational interviews**, which give you the opportunity to learn more about working in a particular industry or job category. You might learn directly from an experienced worker's perspective, for example, that what you thought was exciting in the area of public relations entails long hours, including evenings or weekends, and lots of travel, which would not suit your family life. Or you may feel the chance to travel is what you've always wanted. This type of interview is not job-specific, but broadens your information base, so you can make better career choices and be better prepared when you do go for actual job interviews. Also talk to younger employees (fairly recent alumni) whose experiences at the entry level anticipate more closely what yours might be like.

☐ Engage in internships. As noted in the section on junior year, these are a good way to test the waters in a field of interest, build a résumé, and build your networks. The career office can help you find and obtain internships, but you may also hear of them through campus organizations, through your department, and on the Web.

☐ Use résumé services to be sure that yours is polished and professional, and maximizes your opportunities. You may have mistakenly excluded your role in student government or your volunteer work—these can be more revealing than your stint at Starbucks, in terms of your leadership abilities. The career office picks up on such items. They will also review your **cover letter**, which is crucially important.

☐ Watch for a career week when employers in the area come to your campus and recruit for jobs. You should dress for success and bring copies of your résumé. This is not a gum-chewing, baggy-jeans moment. Recruiters are seriously looking for viable talent, and you should present yourself at your professional best, even when you know that the work environment may end up being more casual.

The Search

☐ Keep an eye on all kinds of websites, want ads, and job boards for opportunities. Use the online and actual job boards or listings your school offers. Also check sites such as **Monster.com**, **HigherEdJobs.com**, **www.idealist.org**, and other targeted sites. You can search by geographic area, job title, or other criteria. If you can be flexible about location, do so. Some parts of the country have more options available than others and may have more in fields of interest to you. Some fields such as the film industry or oil industry just about require that you be in specific geographic areas. Absolutely look at small- to midsize-growth firms, where you may be able to shine sooner. You can gain valuable experience and even expand your horizons with the firm. Check lists such as the *Inc.* magazine 500, where you can find information on growing companies: **www.inc.com/inc500/2009/index.html**.

☐ Take every opportunity to **network**. Whenever you get a chance to talk to someone about your career interest, do it. You may have conversations with a customer in your field whom you see regularly at your Dunkin' Donuts job, or you may make more formal contact through social networking sites such as Facebook or LinkedIn. Certainly talk to your instructors or administrators who know you well. Go to conferences or events related to your field. Try to meet the guest speakers at these events. A guest speaker can open all kinds of doors for students who are poised and confident and approach with an eye to learning more. If you're shy, take the speaker's business card, and then send a note or email of thanks for the presentation, include a question, request a networking interview, or just introduce yourself. Just be sure that your communication is polished and brief. Volunteer to help at events—charity events, for example, can link you to individuals who may be helpful and can also add to your résumé. Even shows like *Good Morning America* now have job-related websites. Up to 85 percent of jobs come through personal contacts. The more persons you know and who know you, the better off you are.

☐ Research **salary levels** for your field of interest. You have to be realistic and prepared for what may be typically low salary levels for entry-level positions. If you come in with great grades and lots of experience from summer jobs and internships, you may be able to get a bit more, but as a new college graduate, you are starting at the lower end of the job ladder, and that means lower pay scales. At the same time, salary levels vary widely. Some industries or job titles pay more and vary by geography. For example, **About.com**'s salary finder shows that an accountant in New York City makes on average six thousand dollars more than one in Denver. But the cost of living is different in the two areas. Armed with this information, you can more clearly assess, if you get a low salary offer, whether you may be facing race or gender discrimination (or just a lowball offer), and you know better how to negotiate upward if you can.

☐   Look into the culture and reputation of a company. Reading trade publications and blogs can help, but also check the lists of best companies to work for that are annually published by *Working Woman*, *Fortune*, and *Black Enterprise* magazines. They may yield insights into the kinds of firms where you would best fit. And, again, talk to employees or former employees of the companies you're exploring.

☐   Target jobs and employers of interest once you've done your research on them. Plan to send out many letters and résumés. Your cover letter should show that you've done your homework on the field and the firm, from your informational interviews and reading of trade publications and blogs. Use these letters to show the match between your background and the firm or field you're trying to get into. Be enthusiastic about your interest in the firm, job, or industry. These materials also act as samples of your writing, so do them well and have others look them over for typos or other errors. In your research, look for the key person at the hiring firms, whether in Human Resources (HR) or the head of the department you're interested in. **Address your letters specifically** to that person. Indicate that you will follow up in a week and then do just that. (But do not overdo the follow-up—that works against you.)

☐   In some cases, you may come across a hard copy or online **application form**. As with grad school applications, these must be filled out with great care and attention to detail. Some areas may be personally tricky for you. If you do not have a green card or visa or if you have been incarcerated, ask your career counselor how to handle these issues. They may not be insurmountable, but they may limit your choices. By law, there are areas that employers are not allowed to question, including your marital status, whether you have (or plan to have) children, your age, ethnicity, or religion. (These can't be asked about in interviews either.)

☐   Employers do **background checks** of various sorts. You should clean up your Facebook and MySpace pages, so that if an employer checks on you, nothing that can put you out of the running for a job because they cast you in an embarrassing light or reflect (youthful?) poor judgment. Also, instead of something such as studmuffin@myself.com, change your email address and voice mail messages to ones that are professional (use your name or initials). Employers also check your credit ratings to see if you are financially responsible. Obviously, for certain jobs there may be questions or checks on any brushes with the justice system. If you're an ex-offender, then be sure to tap organizations that are geared to help you reenter the workplace. Many public colleges also have special programs to support you.

☐ Practice your **interviewing skills**. Your career office may offer practice interviews, or you may just have to ask friends to practice with you. Sometimes professors or others who are invested in you will help out. There are standard questions you might expect. Google "job interview questions," and a host of sites offering interviewing advice appear. Expect an interviewer to ask, for example, why you want the job, what your strengths and weaknesses are, what you are most proud of, or what has been your biggest challenge. Strategies exist for responding in ways that cast you in the best light. Showing your energy and enthusiasm, as well as revealing your skills, can give you an edge over a more experienced candidate. Again, do your homework in preparing for the interview. Don't forget that interviewers also likely ask whether you have any questions. You should have at least two that reflect the research you've done on the firm and the field. Never ask about benefits or salary until there is an offer or you are further along in the process. Again, your career office can help you with this.

☐ Prepare for phone interviews as well. Search consultant Marilyn Machlowitz suggests that you dress for a phone interview as though you were meeting in person and also that you have the website of the firm up in front of you. Have your résumé and cover letter at hand too. Smile while you're on the phone—it shows in your voice. End the conversation with a verbal handshake, such as "I enjoyed speaking with you."

☐ First impressions are a make-or-break moment. Think like the employer, who is envisioning your impact on customers or colleagues. It's important that you have a firm handshake, good eye contact, and a friendly smile. Aim for looking as though you fit in and are likeable. Be sure that the suit or dress you wear is one that makes you feel good and at ease—it should add to your self-confidence. Have an **"interview suit"** in your closet. It should be dark gray, black, or navy, perhaps brown. It must be clean and conservative in cut (the exceptions to this preference may be the fashion, film, or advertising industries, which favor a bit more creative, though professional, flair). Look at what businesspersons are wearing in publications such as *Fortune*, *Crain's*, *Inc.*, or *Business Week*, which include photos. Accessories—ties, scarves, pieces of jewelry—can add color and personality in an interesting, but not crazy, way. Have your hair well cut and groomed and, for women, your nails done in muted shades or no polish at all. If you don't have much to spend, check resources such as Dress for Success or the Bottomless Closet for women. For men, places like Men's Wearhouse offer good value. Sometimes charity thrift shops offer great, gently worn outfits for little money—look for the shops in high-income neighborhoods for real bargains. No jeans or sneakers, flip-flops, halters, or baggy pants, please!

☐ After the interview, send a **thank-you note** typed on stationary (like your cover letter), wherein you thank each of the persons you met with and again restate your interest in the job and the reason you're a perfect fit. This should be a short letter, but you may include a line or two, for example, that you may not have been able to get into the interview. At the end of the interview, you should have learned the process and timetable for making the hiring decision. Using that timeline, you may want to schedule **follow-up calls** (but again, do not be annoying).

The Offer

☐ If you get an offer, congratulations! But you are not yet done. You must get through the **negotiation process**. In a tight economy, you may just be glad for the offer itself. If you've done your homework, however, and know, for example, that the average salary for a position at your level in this part of the country is $3,000 more than your offer, consider suggesting that you're aware of the difference and wonder if there's wiggle room. If a classmate has just gotten a higher offer for a comparable job and has comparable credentials, then you also have grounds to ask for more. The worst an employer can say is no. Understand, however, that your first job establishes your base pay going forward. If merit or annual salary increases are granted based on percentages, then the higher your base, the higher your increase. Even if you move up in level or to another firm, you build on your base pay, so it's worth it to have as high a base as you can manage. Again, if the economy is tight, then there may not be latitude, and you don't want to risk losing the offer. On the other hand, the firm may be impressed that you are savvy enough to try to take care of yourself and recognize that you would bring that skill to their benefit as well.

☐ During the interview, it is illegal for the employer to ask you about your family circumstances. But once you have an offer, you can ask about flexible schedules, for example, to manage children or other dependent care. Sometimes getting an affirmative reply to that request is more probable than getting more money.

☐ At the time an offer is made, the **benefits package** is also explained. It may include

- health-care plan
- retirement benefits

- vacation and sick leave policies
- transit subsidies
- flexible health-care or child-care spending accounts
- child-care subsidies
- other benefits (cafeteria, gym?)

☐ If the company offers a savings plan and/or credit union, take advantage of it, regardless of how young you are. These are avenues for establishing financial stability for the long term.

☐ Next, call your friends and have a party! In all seriousness, be sure to thank all the individuals who have helped along the way. If teachers or college officials have made introductions or supplied references, let them know of your success. In some ways it is theirs too, and they feel good having a part in launching you. They are more likely to help you (or others) again if you are gracious now. Next it will be your turn to help someone else.

This process is time consuming, and that is why starting early is so important. As you graduate, your best-case scenario has that job in place. That is not going to be realistic if you start the process in April of your senior year!

AFFORDING YOUR NEW LIFE

Even if you've been working all along, you may not have engaged in the same way in the formal economic sector. You may have been underemployed while keeping body and soul together during school, working at low-wage jobs or jobs with few if any benefits. Now, as a college graduate, is when you want to set your financial house in order. No matter how little or how much you are going to earn, you should have a plan for how you will budget your new life. It can lead you to your goals and keep you out of financial trouble.

Go back to the chapter on financial aid and look again at the discussion of **budgeting**. Make a detailed budget, and see how it aligns with your job prospects. It may be that some jobs do not suit your needs, or you may (more likely) have to adjust your lifestyle and expenses to fit your starting salary. Fewer iTunes or meals out may be a solution, or you may need a roommate or two or three. Hard as it may be, try to avoid credit card debt.

You may need to establish a checking account in your own name. Look first at credit unions, which, because they are member-owned and managed, have a reputation for being customer-service oriented, ethical, and less costly. If you go with a big bank, then read the fine print about fees and penalties. Fortunately, new legislation restricts how banks can allow you to or charge you for overdrawing your account. Similarly, credit card companies (banks) no longer allow spending above your credit limit, and they must show on your bills how long it will take to pay off your charges.

Housing is going to be the big factor. You may or may not be able to stay in the same living arrangement you've had all through school, or you may want a change. Even if you're living with your parents, they may expect more of you now in terms of a contribution to the household budget. Certainly if you've been lucky enough to live in campus dorms, you have to find a new place to live.

Craigslist has become a huge source of information about sublets, rentals, and roommates. Alumni networks can help, as well as your church or synagogue, where you're more likely to have some awareness of the persons involved.

If you do have roommates, draw up a clear set of rules about everything from rent payments to sharing food and detergent. Remember, other expenses to be shared include utilities (water, electricity, gas, or cable). You have to make decisions about cell vs. land lines, cable TV, and Internet connections.

When you have your new address, remember to share it with friends, family, and the rest of your world. File a forwarding order at your post office.

Another budget item is **health care**. The good news is that, if you're traditional college-graduate age and your parents now carry you on their policy, the new health-care bill allows them to continue to do so until you're twenty-six, while you establish yourself or complete graduate school. If you have to buy your own insurance, professional associations like the National Association of Social Workers offer insurance, as does the Freelancers Union, for those who work independently in a number of fields. Otherwise, be sure to seek an employer that offers benefits (one such employer is Starbucks).

Health insurance is costly when you have to pick up the tab yourself, but the worst is not having it when you need it. You may be perfectly healthy now, but you can always have a biking accident or fall down on the basketball court. A broken leg can set you back tens of thousands of dollars. Health insurance is worth it in the long run.

Food and transportation are the next big factors you cannot escape. You may need to learn to cook! Is public transportation or a car the most cost-effective and convenient way to commute to work or other responsibilities? Think about parking, fuel, and insurance, as well as car payments. Comparison shop for insurance firms and rates. Websites list gas prices in local areas.

You need new **clothing for work**. Your college wardrobe will not do for the work world. Save the baggy pants, tank tops, and flip-flops for weekends. Regardless of what you may see on TV, "sexy" for women is not appropriate for work, so very short skirts or revealing tops do not enhance the perception of your work performance or your judgment. Some settings require suits for men and dresses or suits for women. Buy a few good pieces (of good fabric) that mix and match, for maximum mileage. Designer outlet stores are a fine bet. Dry-cleaning bills should be part of your budget too.

There is a saying: "You should dress for the job you want, not the job you have." Look at what your supervisor, mentor, or other successful person is wearing, and use that as a standard. Even in a casual setting or on "dress-down days," be more formal—khakis and polo shirts for men, slacks and blouses or sweaters for women. Though the workplace may be more casual than in the past, being sloppy or too revealing is just not professional.

If your job requires a BlackBerry, does the company pay for it? Are there other expenses it covers—meals or reimbursement for work travel? If a friend, family member, or classmate is a tax accountant, learn what may be **tax deductions**. If you're in media, for example, your cable bill could count as a business expense. Unreimbursed travel or meals with a work purpose (noted as such in written policy) may count. Even your job-search expenses can be deductions now and in the future. Regarding deductions, the advice of professionals is best. You do not want to find out that you've underpaid your taxes—rather, refunds are welcome. Moreover, be aware of deductions for children and dependents.

If you have **student loans** (that is most of you), they come due after you graduate. Once you've left school and are a wage earner, your loan repayment begins. Lenders notify you and indicate payment schedules. These also become part of your budget. If you go directly to graduate school, you can defer your undergraduate loans until you complete graduate work. If you are employed in certain programs, domains, or parts of the country—AmeriCorps, for instance, or teaching in rural or urban areas—you may also qualify for loan forgiveness. New federal guidelines have expanded eligibility for such programs. While you're in school, talk to the financial aid office about how this may apply to you once you graduate. Treat the aid office as part of your financial planning team.

There are creative ways to **stretch a budget**. Before you leave school, be sure to sell back any books you don't want, as well as other items a new student might find useful. You get the cash and don't have to carry stuff home you won't need. If friends and family ask about graduation gifts, request gift certificates to places where you can get the clothes or household goods you need. Given tight financial times, many websites offer money tips, ranging from Suze Orman to *Good Morning America*'s Melody Hobson. You can get coupons at **coupons.com** and other sites. Here are a few of my favorite tips:

- Throw a pot-luck dinner party (or brunch). Everyone brings too much and you get to keep and live on the leftovers. Or get Netflix films and make popcorn for an at-home movie night with friends, instead of going out.

- Shop at high-end thrift stores (usually benefiting a local charity or hospital) to find great clothes. Host a clothing or accessories swap with friends to share items you're tired of and get new ones.
- Shop off-season for holiday or other gifts and stash them for later. Look for bargains—flea markets, craft fairs, eBay, and even some charity sites, such as the Breast Cancer Site, have bargains under $20.
- Do a weekly meal plan around one major purchase—a ham or chicken (which then becomes sandwiches, omelets, casseroles, or salad). Try to shop only once a week.
- Share babysitting or barter other skills. If you're willing to cook and someone else will babysit, then both of you win.

Ask your friends and family for their favorite ideas or websites for saving and spending wisely.

As we all know now, jobs don't last forever. Having some savings is wise, in case you need to sit it out for a bit. Prudence is now chic. In some ways, you have probably been living on a tight budget throughout your school years. There is no reason to change the attitude when you're a full-time wage earner. In this way, too, college is a good rehearsal for the rest of your life.

Chapter 11
GRADUATION!

The scene is a huge auditorium filled with all kinds of smiling men and women, young and old. Some have come hours early to be at the front of the lines. Some carry balloons and some carry flowers. You can see the pride on every face. All have cameras at the ready. They jockey for the best seats. When the music starts, you can feel the emotion fill the room.

This is the big goal. All of the information in this book is meant to get you here—to graduation! You have worked hard to earn this degree, and you're not the only one who has invested in the outcome.

You and your family have been looking forward to this day for many years—in some cases, since birth. It is no accident that there are logo onesies or tiny T-shirts sold in college bookstores. I know one baby who was given a teeny T-shirt from every school every member of the family had attended—no high expectations there!

Get ready to celebrate. But before you do, make sure you're ready for the big day.

MET YOUR REQUIREMENTS?

First, you must double-check to be sure you are actually getting the degree you've worked for. Virtually every school by now has a system that lets you check your status toward your degree. When you register for your freshman year and every year thereafter, you have to confirm your expected graduation date. That is the date that determines if you are in the class of 2014 or 2018, for instance. Typically, it is four years after you enter, but increasingly students are taking five or even six years to complete the degree when jobs, transfers, and financial challenges are factored in. You may have the choice of graduating at the end of the fall, spring, or summer term. The cycle of classes is geared to graduations at the end of the spring term, but not all students complete on cycle, so there is a choice.

You must be sure that you've dotted all the i's and crossed all the t's. Did you fulfill all your general education or core requirements? Did you complete the language requirement? Fulfill all the terms of your major and/or minors? This is especially important to check if you've transferred from one school to another. Requirements are different from school to school, and a course fulfilling a requirement at one may not do so at another. Even if you started college years ago, stopped out for a time, and return, requirements may be different now. Do you have the requisite GPA overall and in your major/minor, or in your required subjects? Have you paid all bills, including library fines? My college had a swimming requirement that we had to pass for graduation! Is there another such random activity requirement you need to look at? Again, each school is different—the catalog tells you what is currently needed to graduate. Check on this at the end of your junior year before you register for fall senior classes. Then, if you need to take an extra class, you have the time to do so.

At the end of your senior year, you should know that you're on track to pass all your classes—if not, seek help from your dean. Any problems in this regard can change the graduation date on your diploma. Obviously, do not wait until the week before graduation to find out you're not eligible and that the delay prohibits you from taking part in the festivities. By then your family may have made travel plans, taken time off from work, invited other family members to join in celebrations, bought a gift, and set high expectations for a wonderful day.

A Cautionary Tale: Elissa's Transfer Credits

Elissa was a senior planning to graduate. She had transferred from another college in her junior year and believed that of the many credits accepted from her previous school, some satisfied required courses in her new school. Her departmental major advisor signed off on her degree audit form, which had to be submitted to the registrar for graduation. A month before the great event, the registrar reported that a course Elissa thought had fulfilled a writing requirement did not. Elissa was able to show, however, that one of her previous school courses did meet the writing requirement, because she had kept the syllabus. When she appealed the decision concerning her graduation eligibility, she also had in her favor her advisor's error in approving her audit form. So she went from panic to assurance that she could indeed graduate as planned.

Lessons learned: Check and double-check that you have met all requirements, and keep all relevant documents.

We need to distinguish here between graduation as a ceremony and as meeting a legal standard. The reality is that most schools let you march at graduation even if you have a course or two to complete and a plan to get them done immediately. If there is a significant lapse, such as an undone senior thesis paper, then you may have to defer graduation. Each state sets forth rules for academic standards and may mandate the number of credits that must be fulfilled to walk at graduation.

So even though at the ceremony, the college president says something like, "By the powers vested in me by the state of Nebraska, I now declare you graduates of the University of Nebraska," you do not actually get a degree unless you are certified by the registrar as having completed all obligations, academic and otherwise. If the process is done in a timely fashion, you may get the degree that day. If the school allows leeway until the last hour for students to complete their requirements and for last grades to be tallied, then they mail you the degree within a month or so. You may march at graduation, but not get the official degree until sometime later, when all requirements are fulfilled and verified. Once you have the degree in hand, you have actually graduated.

ACTIVITIES AND TRADITIONS

Graduation involves more than just the one ceremony. Many activities and traditions are observed and many matters considered in the run-up to the big day. Leading up to these final festivities, you must pay attention to anywhere from a year's to a week's worth of deadlines and activities. Career Services or Student Activities may hold special workshops throughout the year, focusing on everything from financial planning to finding housing. At the end of the year there may be a Senior Week or just senior activities to lead up to graduation.

Important components of the activities are the dates to buy **class rings** (or other items), order the **yearbook** if your school has one, get tickets for graduation, and take photos in your cap and gown. Your class ring can be a signal to others of where you went to school and a source of pride. The rings may feature a jewel; at the least, they have the school logo or saying, and the date of your graduation. They are not typically cheap (think a few hundred dollars), so if you want one, you have to factor the cost into your senior-year budget. One of the main companies producing rings is Jostens, and their website gives an indication of price ranges.

Photos are an especially important keepsake for your family members. Be sure your hair and makeup are perfect. You are asked to sit for several poses and given a choice of which photos you want to buy and in what sizes. If you did this in high school, you know the drill already. If your school has a yearbook, your photo is included, but images may also be placed on your Facebook page, graduation announcements, or a press notice for your local newspaper. Some schools take photos of each graduate receiving the degree at the ceremony. You will want to keep that memory of you in your cap and gown, with pride.

The yearbook, like yours from high school, is a keepsake of photos of your classmates and memorable events during your time in school—ranging from theater productions to sporting events and random activities. It is another item for the senior-year budget. These days, you may have an e-yearbook online. As an alumnus, you may refer to it years later to see how you and your friends and classmates looked back in the day. It may be where some of your accomplishments and activities are reflected. Some schools include home addresses of the graduating class to make contact easier, though these may be on the alumni Web page as well. The yearbook may reference noteworthy events of a national or local nature that had an impact on you and your classmates: wars, floods, elections. To that extent, it is a kind of time capsule of these years and worth having. You may even be one of the team that puts it together.

Tickets for graduation are a huge source of stress and contention, as few schools have the space to accommodate all the students, faculty, family members, and friends who might like to attend. The school may ask you how many tickets you need up to a limit, or they may offer an exact number, which can be as few as two. As soon as you know your school's rules, let your friends and family know, so they can make arrangements. If you have more family than tickets, see which of your friends may have spares because their families may not be able to travel or get off from work. For both planning and security reasons (especially if there are famous guests, honorees, or speakers), schools are now quite strict about the dispersal of tickets.

The event may be indoors or out, depending on space available and traditions. An outdoor service may allow for more persons to attend, but the weather can be a huge factor. I have sat, soggy under umbrellas, as speakers under a tent went on and on, and I have been freezing during inclement spring weather. On a hot day, students are tempted to wear shorts under their warm robes. Families are certainly advised to prepare for weather at outdoor events. Indoor services restrict the numbers that can take part, especially at large schools, and there can be restrictions on bringing in balloons or other items. Guests should plan to be at the venue a good hour before the event begins, to line up for seats, go through security if needed, find seats, and settle down.

You should think carefully about bringing children to graduation, whether your own or those of siblings or other family or friends. They are often the motivation for going to school, and you want them present at this special moment. At the same time, however, these events are crowded and, for young ones, boring, given the length of time children are expected to sit still and be quiet. I have seen grandmothers or husbands have to miss the main moment because of a crying or fussy baby. If you can leave children home or with a sitter, that may be best, but you know your own family and what is the optimal situation.

Let the school's graduation planners help you with any family member or friend who needs **special accommodations**, such as wheelchair seating or signing for someone who is deaf. Security is also able to help in the event of a health crisis. Individuals have been known to faint, or pregnant guests to go into labor. Schools are ready for these contingencies, based on years of experience.

Several kinds of graduation-related events may take place. Most happen around the spring graduation ceremonies—common is a prom or other big social activity involving the entire school or just a division or department. Colby College in Maine has a clambake for graduates and their families. Students themselves plan events as well, including dances or pub crawls. (Once more, a caution about the binge drinking that is so common at this time of celebration. A special event can become a tragedy at the pop of a beer can.) Some colleges have traditions that go back many generations. Some are serious ceremonies and some amusing (for example, the late-night senior skinny-dip in the Bryn Mawr cloister pond, reportedly begun by Katherine Hepburn, that once resulted in purple seniors when a chemistry grad student put purple dye in the pool).

Departments often throw parties for their graduates and families. These present excellent opportunities for your family to meet the professors they have heard so much about (good or bad!). Professors are inclined to say really nice things about you to your family then, too.

Preplanning includes finding flights, hotels, or rooms for family coming from out of town. You may have to do this as early as a year in advance. As noted, there may be more than one day of festivities or ceremonies, so you may need several days' worth of rooms. It is an additional budget item, but remember that this is a once-in-a-lifetime event, the culmination of all these years of hard work. Websites for graduation should include directions to the campus or the ceremony venue, information on parking, and the nearby restaurants that can accommodate large groups (also to be booked ahead of time). I know families that have rented a van to bring everyone together.

GRADUATION DAY!

Some schools have graduations twice a year, for winter and spring. Very few have anything planned for the students who complete their degree work in the summer. Those students may march either in the spring or the winter. No matter the season, plan to go to the ceremony. This is part of what you have earned. There is a wonderful energy in the air that you do not want to miss. You also do not want to deprive your family members or friends of the chance to celebrate with you and to share in the happiness around your completion of this important goal. They have most likely contributed time, money, or emotional support, and deserve to share the moment with you.

The various kinds of events held can be determined by the size of the school and some by tradition. At a large university such as NYU, Michigan, or UCLA, where there are several colleges within the university, a baccalaureate service and/or a graduation or commencement ceremony are held. The baccalaureate event is for the specific college and allows for a more intimate ceremony, with personal recognition of students, inclusion of all faculty, and perhaps a student speaker from the college. Depending on the scale and the planning horizon, degrees may be given out during the service, or sometimes a rolled and ribboned paper proxy; the real thing comes in the mail later. College-wide or departmental special events may be held, where awards are given out.

The most prominent speakers appear at the main commencement or graduation service. They may be the President of the United States, popular entertainers, businesspersons, or famous alumni (who could in fact be any of the above). The college president speaks, and perhaps deans or the provost speak as well. Besides the main speaker, noteworthy individuals, sometimes alumni and sometimes not, may be given an **honorary degree** acknowledging their contributions to society. These honorary doctorates signify that the work they have done in their lives is equivalent to the learning achieved and recognized by the doctoral degree. Comparable to the main speaker, they may be astronauts, political figures, authors, artists, and sometimes prestigious scientists and professors who've made special contributions in their fields.

Particular student achievements are often recognized. One of the main honors is being chosen the **valedictorian**, the student who has earned the top place in the class by virtue of an exceptional GPA and perhaps a factor related to service. This is a major honor. Even later in life, it is a credential that can be cited. The administration makes the selection, and in the case of GPAs that are very close, they may look at the rigor of courses taken, the number of majors and minors, and any departmental honors. Typically this student is selected to speak on behalf of her or his classmates at graduation. Often the administration also chooses a "runner-up," the **salutatorian**, who also manifests academic and other excellence and may also speak or be acknowledged. These students, along with key administrators, members of the board of trustees, honorary degree recipients, key faculty, and other noteworthy students form the **platform party**, which sits in front of the audience of graduates, families, and friends.

Many elements of graduation are considered traditional "pomp and circumstance." One is the processional song itself, popularly known as "Pomp and Circumstance," which is Edward Elgar's March no. 1. Its title is taken from a line in Shakespeare's *Othello*:

> *Farewell the neighing steed, and the shrill trump,*
> *The spirit-stirring drum, the ear-piercing fife,*
> *The Royal banner, and all quality,*
> *Pride, Pomp, and Circumstance of glorious war!*

When the stanzas of that music begin, everyone knows that the ceremonies are about to start, and the students and platform party march in. The faculty, VIPs, and administrators are in what is called traditional academic attire. Their caps and gowns, like those of many of the graduating students, are of particular colors and include hoods and caps that indicate various meanings, such as the school from which each has graduated. (The University of Indiana is red, the University of Washington blue, and NYU purple.)

Info: Academic Attire

- The **bachelor's gown** you wear is designed to be worn closed (though in the past they were worn open), and all are at least mid-calf length to ankle length.
- The **master's gown** sleeve hangs down in the typical manner, and it is square cut at the rear part of the oblong shape. The front part has a slit for the wrist opening, but the rest of the arc is closed. This gown is designed to be worn open or closed.
- **Doctoral robes**, worn by most faculty, are typically black, although some schools use robes in the school's colors. The outside shell of the hood is black in that case, however. In general, doctoral gowns are similar to those worn by bachelor's graduates, with the addition of three velvet bands

on the sleeves and velvet facing running down the front of the gown, tinted the color designated for the field of study in which the doctorate is awarded. The robes have full sleeves, instead of the bell sleeves of the bachelor's gown.

- Members of the **Board of Trustees or other governing body officers** of a college or university, regardless of their degrees, are entitled to wear doctor's gowns, faced only with black velvet and black velvet bars on the sleeves. Their hoods, however, may represent only a degree actually held by the wearer, or one specially prescribed by the institution. The color for the outside shell of the hood is standardized as black, providing flexibility of use and helping to facilitate this practice.

- In most American colleges and universities, the color of the velvet hood trim worn by the **faculty** is distinctive of the academic field to which the degree pertains—or as closely related as possible. For instance, one who has earned a master's in journalism would wear crimson velvet trim to signify this field, rather than white to convey arts.

The program booklet includes not only the program flow and information on honorees, but also the listing of graduates, clustered by school or discipline, and in alphabetical order. Noted are special honors, fellowship winners, and other forms of recognition for outstanding academic performance by students. You can find your own name there—the booklet is a keepsake of the occasion. Be aware that this is also a reason you should know your eligibility to graduate and to march, so that your name makes its way into this printed document.

Following the processional, the ceremony usually begins with an invocation or prayer by a religious figure affiliated with the school or prominent in the community. Once the speeches are done and the honors and degrees conferred, the same or a similar figure likewise closes the ceremony with a benediction. The service can end with a lively piece of music that could be the school song or another popular song that captures the spirit of the moment. As the platform party of faculty and officials marches out, mayhem begins. At Annapolis and West Point, hats fly into the air. At NYU, students dunk in the Washington Square Fountain. Everyone is cheering, and balloons or confetti may fly. It is a time of tears—of joy, sometimes of sorrow at leaving friends. Every school has its own traditions, but at every school there are hugs and forms of celebration all around.

This is an event that represents your accomplishments and the launch of your future—hence the word "commencement"—a beginning and not an end. You should be proud that you have done the work and met the challenges. Revel in every part of your achievement with those you love who have supported you along the way. This is your time. Congratulations, graduate!

Chapter 12
BEING AN ALUMNUS

What a joy to be able to say, "I am a college graduate!" That is a hard-won accomplishment and just to say it is a source of happiness and pride. Your school, however, also wants to hear you say that you are a Howard graduate or a Boston College graduate. They want to see that school sticker on the back of your car forever (or at least until your kids start college). They certainly want you to give money to the school, but they know that usually doesn't happen until you're really established. The main thing is they want you to feel pride in what your college has provided for you.

You may not even begin to realize the value of your education until years later. If you've had to struggle or are just exhausted, you may not have those warm, fuzzy feelings for a long time. As your career moves forward, however, you may find that reading, problem solving, or research skills are the ones propelling you forward. The discipline you gained in managing a full schedule and getting papers done on time while helping with campus elections is what makes it possible for you to multitask at work and put in a lot of hours. The capacity for leading others, which you didn't know you had, but which surfaced when you were asked to help orient new students, shows up as you lead a team of coworkers in a project.

In either case, embrace being an alumnus. The benefits of being an alumnus are twofold: the networks you formed and the institutional ties. Both are the responsibility of the **Alumni Affairs office**, and typically, you can access an alumni website to learn more about the benefits and activities you may find of interest. An **alumni association** is usually an independent structure, whose governance is separate from that of the college. You should definitely join—any dues or fees for membership are minor compared to the value of what you get as a graduate.

A Story: Eleanor

Eleanor decided twenty years after graduating from college to return to school for a doctorate. At a pre-reunion event, she ran into a classmate who had gone on to work as a book editor, and the two, who had not been part of the same crowd at college, discovered that they lived in the same area and had many common interests. As Eleanor struggled to complete her 350-page dissertation, her classmate *volunteered* to edit Eleanor's work. It was a true gift and labor of love.

YOUR COLLEGE NETWORK

You may meet your roommate or the person sitting next to you at orientation and become best friends on the spot, for life. But even though that is rare, it is not uncommon for you to find individuals in your early days or weeks who do stay with you for a lifetime. My mother's college roommate was her best friend until she died some sixty-five years later. My son's best friends are from college, as is his wife. If you are in a commuter college, it's easy to go to classes and go home or to work and not connect with anyone. That is a mistake. Those you meet in college are sharing a similar experience with you, one not shared by family— often not even by friends. You may find that you come from similar backgrounds or neighborhoods and so can have the same perspective on your college life. You have the chance to commiserate or support each other through challenging times. Once you've graduated, you also meet others with similar experiences who can be enormously important to you. Note that websites such as Facebook and LinkedIn focus on alumni ties, and specific school networks may be on the sites.

There are class reunions—sometimes every year, sometimes every five, depending on your college and its traditions. These can take many forms: a one-day event or, sometimes for large urban schools, a reception and dinner. Or they may be a full weekend of activities, including lectures, dinners, entertainment, and campus tours, complete with child care and events for spouses. You may experience lovely traditions involving music, such as the step sings of many women's colleges, or curious events such as the Princeton "P-rade," when each class walks wearing unique orange-and-black jackets designed for the class. Each class may have a party or dinner, and sometimes favorite faculty members are invited. You should plan to attend a reunion at least once.

Many find it reassuring to discover that nearly everyone in their cohort has been dealing with similar life experiences, whether career- or family-related. If your class members are widely dispersed, coming together with others who've shared the time and space of your college life can help break the isolation from one another. It's not unusual to find that you can become closer after graduation to persons you didn't know well in college. You may have similar careers or life experiences. Maybe you never had a chance to connect in school, but find each other at reunion, and something clicks.

The interesting conversations about issues and ideas that kept you hanging around after class or in the halls or awake in the dorms may not be happening in your life as often after school ends. Those important exchanges may have been a source of stimulation and energy, and even reassurance that you were an intelligent being. Reunions can revive those feelings and discussions. You can keep them going using Facebook, Google, or Yahoo! groups.

At reunions or other college alumni events, you can build your career through crucial networking in a less formal environment, one where people are familiar with your background and training because they share it. Some colleges actually sponsor career networking events for alumni. Others may hold events for undergraduates where alumni take part, and where you can take the opportunity to meet fellow alumni in your field. For example, a careers panel on the law puts you in contact with other lawyers. Committees related to alumni activities—say, on ethnic affairs or international travel opportunities, scholarship allocations, or even the selection of a new college president—could enhance your networks and also provide the gratification of connecting with individuals you respect. Certainly leadership opportunities exist related to the class or to raising funds for the college. All of this kind of participation keeps your name and image fresh in the minds of others. If you look around, you'll see that firms often end up employing numbers of individuals from particular schools—that is because people like to work with those they know or trust, and the "old school tie" confers a sense of common background over and above your origins.

Info: Alumni Association Roles

Some roles you may play as an alumnus are

- **Class president**—keeps the class connected to the college and represents its point of view on matters of policy affecting alumni.
- **Class secretary**—keeps track of the class members and provides updates for websites or alumni publications; may also keep records of meetings or votes engaged in by the class.
- **Treasurer** or **fund-raising chair**—helps raise funds from the class for the college, but may also have a role in planning events and activities and raising funds needed for them.
- **Reunion chair**—helps to organize reunion activities for the class.
- **Board of Trustees**—the governing body for the college. While there may be non-alumni on the board, it is typically made up of the most prestigious alumni, those who can raise

money, or those who have demonstrated strong leadership and love of the school.

- **Advisory boards or committees**—can be created to support particular initiatives relating to career services or scholarship activities, or even athletic teams.

Raising money for your school is a key expectation and responsibility for alumni. If you received a scholarship named for an individual, that person likely had a connection to an alumnus or was an alumnus. The family of a graduate who died may create a scholarship fund to commemorate that person. Most often a graduate may, in his or her will, leave funds to help other students get through. When a graduate becomes the head of the biggest new business, a campus may be pleasantly surprised by a generous gift. Sometimes students who have struggled want to ensure that others don't have the same experience, and so contribute scholarship money. The funds for prizes are usually also the result of bequests or gifts from alumni. As you go around your campus, you notice buildings, classrooms, or other features named for individuals—these too are often gifts from alumni.

In the early years after graduation you may not have much to give, so pooling your funds with your classmates' may add up to significant and useful amounts to the college. Alumni most often might be interested in donating for scholarships, but colleges have other needs as well—funds for what are called "capital projects" (new or refurbished buildings, books for the library). You may not be able to give every year, but give when you can. It is paying back for what you've gotten and paying forward for future generations.

As you progress through life and climb up your career ladder, your accomplishments may come to the attention of your college's alumni affairs office. You may be selected for a hall of fame, given recognition on the college website, asked to speak at events, mentor students, or even speak at graduation, if you reach high levels of success. You can add such recognition to your résumé, as well as the work you do for your college in a formal way (on committees, for example). These are continuing affirmations of the kind of person you are and how well you are perceived by others. Your college wants you to be a proud alumnus, but it also revels in the opportunity to be proud of you!

ALUMNI RESOURCES

As an alumnus you are able to derive benefits that go beyond networking and the quality of your education. You may be able to keep, for life, the college email address you were given, or the school may forward any messages to your personal email. This makes it easy to stay in touch with other alumni. These are just a few of many ways colleges continue to support you long after you've graduated. You may have to pay a small fee or membership dues in the alumni association, but it is worth it if you do. Often schools issue alumni a special ID that gives access to various places and services around campus.

One of the most important resources is the career services office, which may be free or covered in your alumni dues. Be sure to sign up to get email notifications of career events and activities that you are eligible to attend. Lehigh and Notre Dame, for example, have outreach programs to help alumni find jobs when they've lost them. When you're changing careers or in a downturn, career services can help you revamp your résumé, share job opportunities for experienced workers, and guide you to other alumni who can be helpful. If you go to the open market for career guidance, you can expect to pay hundreds of dollars. You should know by now that you can access these school resources for the rest of your life, for close to no charge. They know that once you're back on your feet, you'll be a loyal and grateful contributor.

If, for graduate school applications or even job searches, you need the letters of recommendation faculty wrote for you, you may be able to access them through the registrar, the career office, or even the deans, for some period of time, though not always indefinitely. Over the years I have been impressed by the extent to which employers contact career offices looking for candidates with five or more years of experience—that is to say, alumni.

There may also be other events of interest. Campuses are wonderful places to hear public officials, political figures, and others prominent in the news media, often for free. Student art shows, as well as performances in theater, dance recitals, or concerts take place. The presence of an auditorium or theater also means that professional groups may appear for little cost. Some campuses present programs for children on weekends, which can be great low-cost family entertainment.

Some colleges have facilities that you can rent for your own events. These generate income for the school, but may cost little. Alumni and/or faculty clubs can be on or off campus; they often offer meals, facilities for overnight stays, and space for receptions or meetings with other alumni. Membership fees are far less costly than most private clubs and can provide a wonderful venue for meeting with clients or others in a prestigious environment. If there is a chapel or another site of great beauty on campus, alumni sometimes marry there. If you and your intended both have strong ties to the school, then the event becomes a bit of an ad hoc reunion.

Although not typically inexpensive, college travel groups offer alumni, usually older ones, the chance to travel accompanied by a professor knowledgeable about the destination. On a trip to the Middle East, China, or Italy, let's say, an expert (or two) shares insights about the politics, art, or culture of the region, and you learn more than you would on your own or with other types of groups. You also have the benefit of intelligent discussion with other classmates or alumni as you tour.

Back on campus, using your alumni ID card, you usually have library privileges, which can be useful for research projects related to your trips or other interests, and you can access magazines or journals you don't want to subscribe to.

Colleges also offer financial benefits to alumni, in some cases. You can obtain "affinity cards" from large schools like the University of Michigan. These are normal credit cards (Visa/MasterCard) that carry the college logo and give a small percentage of profit to the alumni association or college.

Some schools—my own campus, Bryn Mawr, for one—offer low-cost term life insurance policies for alumni. The alumni association functions as a "group" for the purposes of the insurance pool.

An alumni website is the tool that connects you to other classmates and gives you a sense of their locations and activities. It may even offer ways to post want ads or other queries. Although the format is probably on the decline now, a school alumni directory can provide a compendium of information about students from the time the school began keeping records. It can include local address, marital status, children, place and address of employment, and other information—all supplied by the individuals with their permission.

You may have heard the term "legacy" children. These are the children of alumni; they are often given a special look when they apply to the colleges their parents attended. My stepdaughter was a "legacy" at Bryn Mawr. Your child must meet the requirements of the college (SAT/GPA), but the school considers it a courtesy to its alumni to pay extra attention to their children. It is an affirmation of how the alumnus enjoyed and benefited from his or her time there. It is truly exciting when your child can follow in your footsteps, especially when you have been the first in the family to go to college or are among few of your background on a prestigious campus.

While the financial benefits or a lecture series are wonderful rewards, the best alumni benefit is always the connection with others who can support you as you go through life. College is difficult, and these are the persons who weather that intense period with you. Take advantage of all the tools to which your alumni status entitles you, especially the ones that help you remain tied to the individuals who made it possible for you to get through—your classmates.

A PARTING NOTE

As the world of work has become more complex, and demands for higher and higher skill levels have emerged as essential to advancement, college has replaced high school as the educational level most necessary in order to succeed. The pressure to attend college has become enormous and the competition fierce; the anxiety extends beyond the college door into the life of the student. The worry can become so paralyzing that, whatever the cause, many students stumble at some point and are not able to regain their footing. The result is the increasing number of students who drop out and decide that college is not for them—thus closing off the many opportunities that higher education provides. We have shown you that there is an alternative to this scenario.

It is my hope that this book has provided you with the tools and information you need to achieve the most crucial goal: to stick with it and graduate from college, and by doing so, to become a more literate, tolerant, informed, analytical, creative human being. If nothing else, I hope you understand that *asking questions and finding the right persons to support you are the most important things you can do to ensure your success*—both in college and in life. College teaches you how to do this, giving you ways to overcome your fears or preconceptions about such ideas, as well as lessons for living. If you navigate beyond the barriers of bureaucracy and overcome your own fears of the unknown, you find the college experience to be one of the best and most rewarding of your accomplishments over a lifetime. It is the gateway to achievement, to a richer life—both materially and intellectually—and it is the source of relationships that are meaningful for decades after. You *CAN* finish college! May you graduate, thrive, and live with the pride of achievement!

INDEX

W

Withdrawing from a class, 79–81, 188–189
Work-study, 120
Writing and communication skills, 64, 69, 93, 94–95, 136, 162, 177–181

Y

Yearbooks, 236, 237